JUNG

JUNG

ANTHONY STORR

ROUTLEDGE
NEW YORK

The cover illustration is taken from The Archetypes & the Collective Unconscious by C.G. Jung, in the Collected Works of C.G. Jung Vol 9:1.

Published in USA in 1991 by Routledge
An imprint of
Routledge, Chapman and Hall Inc.
29 West 35 Street
New York, NY 10001

First published in the Fontana Modern Masters Series in 1973

Library of Congress Cataloging-in-Publication Data

Storr, Anthony.
    [C.G. Jung]
    Jung / Anthony Storr.
        p.   cm.
    Reprint. Originally published: C.G. Jung. New York : Viking, 1973.
    Includes bibliographical references.
    ISBN 0-415-90411-0 (pbk.)
    1. Jung, C. G. (Carl Gustav), 1875-1961.   2. Psychoanalysis.
I. Title.
[BF109.J8S76   1991]
150.19'54 — dc20   90-47027
                    CIP

Contents

Preface to the Routledge Edition

This book was first published in 1973 by Fontana in England and Viking in the U.S. I came to write it as the consequence of a chance encounter. I went to a literary party at the Ritz Hotel in London which was given for C.P. Snow, and found myself standing next to Frank Kermode, whom I already knew. "You edit the Modern Masters Series don't you?" I asked. "Yes," he replied. "Who is writing the one on Jung?" I inquired. "No-one," he said. "Would you like me to write it?" "Yes," said Frank Kermode. And so it came about. I remember that Kermode altered my first sentence; but I don't think he made any other emendments.

I was fortunate enough to meet Jung on one occasion in 1951, at the time when he was engaged in writing *Answer to Job.* His friend Dr. E.A. Bennet, who arranged the interview for me, impressed upon me the importance of making notes of what Jung said. With some reluctance, I did so immediately after the interview was over. Those notes, which I still have, proved very useful when I later wrote the book.

In person, Jung was a very tall, powerfully built man, who was proud of his strength and who retained his vitality and appetites into extreme old age. He was completely without pomposity, and had an admirable sense of humor. He was well aware of his exceptional gifts and learning, and was far too realistic to exhibit any false modesty. But he was the least pretentious of men, and for this reason was able to make an immediate and genuine contact with those who came to see him. There was a tough, earthy quality about Jung which may have surprised those who had expected to find a mystic. No man knew more than he did of the aspirations of the human spirit; but no man was more rooted in reality or more obviously enjoyed the physical pleasures. To meet him was to feel that to be fully human could be an exciting adventure.

In 1959, when Jung was eighty-four, BBC television showed an interview with Jung in their *Face to Face* series, which has since become famous. I am glad to recall that I had a hand in this, since the BBC asked me to brief John Freeman about Jung before he went to Zürich to talk to him. Freeman and his subjects usually became friends; and Jung was no exception. In his introduction to *Man and His Symbols,* Freeman writes: "That was the beginning of a friendship that meant a great deal to me and, I hope, gave some pleasure to Jung in the last years of his life."

When this book was first published, it offended some of the Jungian establishment because I had dared to make some modest criticisms of the Master. More particularly, my friend Gerhard Adler was put out, and reviewed the book somewhat harshly. Those days are now over, and I gather that even dedicated Jungians regard it as a useful introduction. The rift with Gerhard Adler was healed when my book of selections *The Essential Jung* was published by Princeton University Press in 1983. I am proud that Adler, who was one of the joint editors of Jung's Collected Works, should have welcomed this later book as "most competent and reliable." I have sometimes been accused by reviewers of uncritical adulation of Jung, but this is entirely unfounded. All gurus have feet of clay, and Jung was no exception. Jung was a human being, not a saint; and, like other human beings, he sometimes behaved badly. This in no way detracts from the remarkable contributions which he made to psychology and psychotherapy.

1991

1 The Personal Background

This book is primarily about Jung's ideas, and not about the man himself. But since, especially in the realm of dynamic psychology, it is impossible to separate ideas from the personality of the man to whom they occurred, some introductory remarks about Jung as a person are necessary.

Carl Gustav Jung was born on July 26th, 1875. His father was a country parson; a pastor in the Swiss Reformed Church, and also an Oriental and classical scholar. According to Jung's own account, his father was kind, tolerant, and liberal. He was also somewhat conventional; content to accept the system of religious belief in which he had been reared, and unable or unwilling to answer the doubts and queries of his gifted son. Jung describes his father as weak. Indeed, he goes so far as to say that, in childhood, he associated the word 'father' with reliability, but also with powerlessness. There is no doubt, from his own description, that Jung belonged to that not inconsiderable group of creative people springing from families in which the mother is the more powerful and dynamic figure; and this is reflected in Jung's psychological thinking.

In the pages which follow, it is inevitable that Jung's 'analytical psychology' will frequently be contrasted with Freud's 'psychoanalysis'. This is partly because of the close association between the two men, and their subsequent divergence; and partly because the ideas of Freud, so much better known than those of Jung, provide a useful foil or contrast against which to measure the latter.

Jung's mother is described by him as problematical, and also inconsistent, in that she sometimes expressed conventional opinions which another, unconventional part of herself proceeded to contradict; so that the boy early recognized that she did not always say what she really meant, and was thus a divided person. Moreover, when Jung was about three years old, his mother left home to enter hospital for a period of several months suffering from an illness which Jung later attributed to difficulties in the marriage. The little boy responded to this desertion by developing a generalized eczema, a skin disease often considered to be partly emotional in origin. He also developed a deep distrust of women in general, and an ambivalent attitude towards his mother in particular.

In contrast, Freud's mother was warmly protective, and indeed adoring; whereas his father was strict, and undoubtedly the authority in the home. It is not surprising, therefore, that Freudian psychoanalysis is a paternally-based psychology, with a good deal of emphasis upon conscience, duty, and fear of punishment. The Freudian 'superego' is certainly more masculine than feminine. Jungian analytical psychology, on the other hand, is far more rooted in the maternal, and concerned with images of woman as devourer and destroyer as well as protector; concepts which really entered psychoanalysis only with the advent of Melanie Klein. Jung was little concerned with the superego, which indeed he disparages in one passage as an illegitimate construct; but he was very much concerned with the efforts of the developing personality to extricate itself from the toils of maternal encirclement.

Brought up in such a household, and at such a date, it was inevitable that Jung, throughout his life, should have been much preoccupied with questions of religion. In this latter half of the twentieth century it may be diffi-

cult for many younger people to realize how shattering
it was for the orthodox, less than a hundred years ago, to
discover that they had doubts about their faith, or even
worse, might in honesty be forced to abandon it. A
glance, however, at the history of the 'Oxford Movement', at Newman's 'Apologia pro Vita sua', or even at
the letters of Gladstone, will convince the sceptic that
religious problems were the chief preoccupation of some
of the most able minds of the nineteenth century, and
were, moreover, no mere intellectual exercises, but
deeply-felt quandaries which evoked powerful emotions,
and indeed, the whole personality. A good deal of
Jungian psychology can be seen as part of Jung's attempt
to find a substitute for the orthodox faith in which he
was reared, but against which he started to rebel at a
very early age. Freud's parents presented him with no
such problem, since they adhered to the Jewish faith but
tenuously; and Freud was content to be a sceptical
agnostic from childhood onwards.

Jung was brought up in the country; and, in later life,
was at pains to emphasize the good effect this rural
childhood had had upon him; especially in giving him a
healthy attitude to such natural phenomena as birth,
death, and sex. He was also reassured to find that peas-
ants shared his interest in the occult and inexplicable, a
theme which, like religion, continued to crop up in his
writings from his very first paper to his late reflections
on flying saucers. Jung cannot be understood unless it is
remembered that, for him, unlike Freud, natural science
was not enough. There had always to be a background of
something supernatural which could not be explained
away by the rationalism which took hold upon men's
minds at the end of the nineteenth century, and which
appealed so strongly to the hard-headed and somewhat
pessimistic Freud. In his autobiography, Jung writes of
an imperishable world, as opposed to this transitory one.

It is clear that such a world was, for him, always a reality.

At home, Jung remained an only child for the first nine years of his life, when a sister appeared to join him. Although he welcomed the companionship with which his country school provided him, he was far ahead of his companions intellectually, and thus lacked the shared intimacy which can only flourish upon a basis of equality. Jung was a warm-hearted, sympathetic, and compassionate individual; but, judging from what he writes about himself, real intimacy did not come easily to him. The enforced solitude of his childhood was later turned to good account in his self-analysis; but, like many another only child, Jung felt himself to be different from, and to some extent at odds with, his contemporaries. His most important experiences in life came to him when he was alone; and it is characteristic that his autobiography contains next to nothing about his personal relationships. His wife, for instance, is hardly mentioned; the only reference to marriage in the index is 'marriage, mystic of the Lamb', and the only comment on her death is 'After my wife's death in 1955, I felt an inner obligation to become what I myself am.'[1] This predilection for the solitary accounts for the fact that Jungian psychology is principally concerned, not with interpersonal relationships, but with processes of growth and development of personality seen as taking place within the charmed circle of the individual psyche. Freudian psychoanalysis has as its end-point of development a mature relationship with another person, briefly and incompletely designated as 'genitality'; a concept which really includes within it much more than sex. Jung's notion is of an end-point of integration or balance within the individual mind itself, without overt reference to relations with other persons at all.

Jung's original wish was to be an archaeologist. But

his family were poor, and could not afford to send him further afield than Basel, in which city he went to school from the age of eleven. In the University of Basel there was no-one teaching archaeology, so Jung chose medicine instead. With the aid of a grant from Basel University he completed his medical degree, and had almost decided to specialize in surgery when he came across a book by Krafft-Ebing. This was not 'Psychopathia Sexualis', by which this author is principally known to English readers, but a text-book of psychiatry, a subject to which Jung had so far paid no attention. Reading this book convinced Jung that he must specialize in this neglected and poorly-regarded branch of medicine; and his reason for this unexpected decision is worth noting, since it throws light upon the psychological views which he later adumbrated. Krafft-Ebing described psychiatry as being a subject in so elementary a stage of development that text-books upon it were inevitably stamped with the author's subjective assumptions, and tinged by his own personality. This is a reproach which holds good to this day. Instead of being put off psychiatry by reason of this lack of objective, scientific status, Jung was immediately powerfully attracted to it. He was interested in natural science; and well aware of the need for objectivity. But he was also aware of his own internal preoccupation with religious speculation, philosophy, and the search for value and meaning; interests to which it is difficult to apply the strict criteria of science, and in which subjectivity is bound to find a place. It seemed to Jung that psychiatry might fulfil his need to reconcile these opposites within himself; and the reconciliation of opposites is a theme which runs right through the whole of Jung's work. In the case of this particular pair of opposites it is fair to say that he was not entirely successful. On the one hand, Jung refers to his ideas as a subjective confession, thus denying them universal validity. On the other, he writes of the 'objective psyche' (a synonym for the collective unconscious) as a sphere of mental functioning quite removed from personal experience or any trace of subjectivity. No human observer can, of course, be entirely objective, but Jung's reiterated claim that he merely observed facts and tried to classify them often seems at variance with his repeated assertion that no observer can avoid beginning from personal assumptions. Indeed, Jung recognized that the final incompatibility between himself and Freud sprang from the fact that each made observations upon the basis of differing assumptions about human nature.

Whilst still a student, Jung took part in 'table-turning' experiments. The medium, aged $15\frac{1}{2}$, claimed that she received messages from dead relatives and other spirits. One of these spirits spoke almost faultless High German, whereas the girl herself, when in her normal waking state rather than in a trance, spoke only Swiss German. This phenomenon of two apparently quite different personalities manifesting themselves in one girl excited Jung's interest; and his first published work, his dissertation for his medical degree, is a paper 'On the Psychology and Pathology of So-called Occult Phenomena' which is based upon his observations of this girl. I mentioned above that Jung regarded his mother as possessing two personalities; a conventional one, and an unconventional one which sometimes expressed the opposite of what the conventional person had just announced. He very early regarded himself in like fashion. From the age of twelve, he conceived the idea that also consisted of two personalities, one being a schoolboy who was uncertain of himself, solitary, and somewhat ill-at-ease in the world; the other an old man of great authority who commanded respect, who was influential, powerful, and certain of himself. Here, then, are further pairs of opposites, this time manifesting themselves as separate personalities rather than simply as different aspects of the same personality, as in the case of Jung's 'objective' and 'subjective' interests mentioned above.

This tendency to personify and give names to differing aspects of the mind of one person remained with Jung throughout his life. Thus, some of his archetypes, especially the 'anima', 'animus', and 'wise old man' are personified in this way. Moreover, Jung encouraged his patients to conduct dialogues with these 'figures from the unconscious' as if they were real people in the external world. Indeed, to him, they probably were just as real as the persons with whom he came into contact in daily life. The language he uses about such figures suggests that, as mediums believe, he thought of them as existing in an 'imperishable world' and manifesting themselves from time to time through the psyche of an individual. In his autobiography, for example, Jung refers to a figure originating in one of his dreams whom he named Philemon. This figure, Jung writes, taught him psychic objectivity and the reality of the psyche. By holding conversations with him Jung became convinced that Philemon possessed superior insight, and generated thoughts within Jung's mind which he himself would not have been capable of conceiving. Of course, most people, and especially creative people, are well aware that ideas 'come to them', that problems are solved in sleep, and that there are many other manifestations of mental functioning which are not within conscious control or the product of deliberate ratiocination. But very few people find it necessary to personify these 'unconscious' mental activities in the way that Jung did any more than they find it necessary to personify physical parts of themselves like the liver or kidneys, which function independently of the will. Jung's predilection for naming and personifying surely dates from his childhood view of his mother and himself; and from his willingness to accept the medium's view of herself as the spokesman through which superior beings from the 'beyond' made themselves known. This is an aspect of Jungian psychology which some people find irritating, and which may blind them to Jung's more valuable insights.

It is interesting to note, in passing, that both Jung and Freud began their psychological observations upon cases of hysteria; for the 15½-year-old medium would undoubtedly so be diagnosed by a psychiatrist. Freud's studies led him to lay emphasis upon 'repression' in hysteria; that is, the banishment from the consciousness of thoughts and feelings which were distasteful to the conscious ego. For Freud, the ego remained firmly in the driver's seat as the most important part of the personality; and the object of psychoanalysis was to convert id into ego. 'Where id was, there shall ego be.' Jung, although recognizing the validity of repression as a psychological mechanism, attributed more importance to dissociation and splitting within the mind; and tended to treat the split-off portions as alternate personalities, almost of equal importance with the ego, and capable of taking over from it. Cases of 'multiple personality' were beloved of nineteenth-century psychiatrists who encouraged their hysterical patients to continue producing alternative personalities by their injudicious use of hypnosis. Jung, like Freud, soon abandoned hypnosis, but he continued to regard the ego more as one amongst many 'personalities' than as the central directing aspect of the person to which all else ought to be subordinate. One might almost oversimplify by saying that Freud's principal interest was in discovering secrets, whilst Jung's was in reconciling conflicting 'personalities' within the mind.

This emphasis upon dissociation and splitting was reinforced by Jung's clinical experience. After qualification as a doctor, he obtained, in December 1900, a post as an assistant in the Burghölzli mental hospital in Zürich; the city in a suburb of which he was to live for the rest of his life. Here, his interest was engaged by schizophrenia (or 'dementia praecox', as this disorder was then named). He observed that, in schizophrenia, the personality of the patient was not so much divided into two or more clearly distinguishable parts, but rather fragmented: that is, disintegrated rather than merely dissociated. Nevertheless, amongst the fragments, there might be some 'voices' which exhibited a certain continuity with which the therapist could maintain a dialogue. Moreover, Jung noted, as many psychiatrists working in mental hospitals have done since, that the patient's 'ego' might remain more or less intact, although invisible, throughout many years of chronic mental illness. If a chronic schizophrenic becomes physically ill, it sometimes happens that his 'normal' personality, i.e. his ego, reasserts its supremacy, and that he may, therefore, talk and behave ordinarily for a while; only to relapse again when the physical illness has passed. It is difficult to explain this phenomenon in terms of the Freudian mental topography of ego, superego and id, unless one is in the habit of conceiving the ego as more easily split into multiple 'egos' than Freud was prepared to do, at least in his early work.

It was during his time at the Burghölzli also that Jung made some of the observations which led to his hypothesis of a 'collective', as opposed to a merely personal, unconscious. His knowledge of philosophy, comparative religion, and myth led him to make comparisons between this material and the phantasies and delusions of schizophrenics. He found many parallels; and concluded that schizophrenia laid bare, as it were, a deeper level of the mind than could be explained in terms of personal repression and the vicissitudes of early childhood.

In one of his last writings Freud comes close to Jung's point of view when he writes: 'Dreams bring to light material which cannot have originated either from the dreamer's adult life or from his forgotten childhood. We are obliged to regard it as part of the *archaic heritage* which a child brings with him into the world, before any experience of his own, influenced by the experiences of his ancestors. We find the counterpart of this phylogenetic material in the earliest human legends and in surviving customs.'[2]

It is important to realize that much of Jung's thought takes origin from his clinical experiences whilst at the Burghölzli. Freud never worked in a mental hospital for more than a very brief period as a locum tenens, and had little experience with psychotic patients, whom he mostly regarded as quite beyond the reach of psychoanalysis. His original theories were based first upon the phenomena of hysteria, and then upon obsessional neurosis. But Jung's mental hospital experience continued from 1900 to 1909, when he finally resigned from the hospital to pursue his private psychotherapeutic practice. Even then, as we shall see, he did not abandon his interest in schizophrenia; and many of his patients continued to be either borderline psychotics or frankly schizophrenic. Indeed, judging from the paucity of casehistories in the voluminous corpus of Jung's writings, he was not much interested in neurosis as such. After the break with Freud, there are very few neurotic casehistories to be found in all the volumes of the Collected Works; and even in his earlier writings, there are no neurotic case-studies of anything like the complexity of Freud's 'Wolf Man', 'Rat-Man' or 'Little Hans'. Kind and compassionate though Jung was, he was always more interested in ideas than in people, and rapidly became bored with the unravelling of those emotional tangles within the family which constitute the bread-and-butter of the average psychotherapeutic practice.

Jung did much valuable work whilst at the Burghölzli,

some of which I shall later discuss. At this point, however, I am more concerned with how his personal experience bore upon his work and ideas than with the ideas themselves. The next important biographical landmark is his first meeting with Freud. Although Jung had been familiar with Freud's ideas for some years, and had read 'The Interpretation of Dreams' when it first appeared in 1900, he did not actually meet Freud until March 3rd, 1907. Since Jung is often regarded as a renegade Freudian, it is important to recognize that by the time he first encountered Freud, Jung had already had six years psychiatric experience, had produced original work of his own, and had begun, tentatively, as behoved a man still in his early thirties, to formulate some characteristically 'Jungian' ideas which did not accord with Freud's conceptions. That these ideas did not find their full expression until 1913, when Jung finally broke with Freud, is not surprising, when one considers the intensity of the relationship between them. Freudians and Jungians will probably always disagree about the nature of this relation, the former emphasizing it and treating Jung as a heretic; whilst the latter minimize it and possibly believe Jung to have been more independent than, for a time, he was. In fact there were probably powerful emotions on both sides. It must be recollected that Freud was the older man by nineteen years and had already aroused a good deal of controversy by the time Jung met him. At all events, Jung had been warned that it would do his career no good if he continued to support Freud in print, as he did, before they had encountered each other personally, in some early papers. This warning naturally made him defend Freud all the more vehemently; for all of us are apt to be over-enthusiastic about those whom we feel to be rejected unfairly, and on whose behalf we take up the cudgels. It must also be remembered that Jung's respect for his father was

rather slight, although he regarded him with some aff-
ection. He must therefore have been susceptible to
'falling for' an older man whose intellect he could ad-
mire, and who advanced controversial ideas with such
courage. Freud, on his part, was much in need of ad-
vocacy by persons belonging to the psychiatric establishment who were not connected with his immediate
circle in Vienna. Jung was a teacher and research
worker in a famous Swiss mental hospital whose opinion
would be respected by the world at large. Moreover,
unlike the majority of Freud's circle, he was not a Jew,
a point emphasized by Freud himself in a letter to
Ernest Jones. It is no wonder that, for a time, Jung
seems to have become for Freud a favourite 'son', and
Freud, for Jung, a 'father-figure'. Whatever the truth
of this may be, the two men talked enthusiastically for
thirteen hours upon their first meeting, stayed in each
other's houses, and collaborated as best they could by
letter and occasional encounters at conferences and
meetings. In Vol. IV of Jung's Collected Works, 'Freud
and Psycho-Analysis', the fertilizing effect of this collaboration at a distance is evident. So also is the fact that
there were areas of disagreement from the beginning.
Whatever Jung's feelings for Freud may have been, he
was never an uncritical disciple, although, as he himself
admitted, he suppressed his criticisms and set aside his
own judgement during the period of their collaboration.
Whilst writing his book 'The Psychology of the Unconscious', later to be called 'Symbols of Transformation',
Jung became aware that some of his conceptions differed
so radically from those of Freud that it was likely that
the publication of them would lose him Freud's friendship. This idea disturbed Jung to such an extent that he
was unable to proceed with his writing for two months;
a fact which attests the emotional importance to him of
his relation with Freud. Writing, it may be observed, is a

solitary occupation in which the writer is often attempting to clarify his own point of view uncontaminated by the influence of others. It is clear that, in writing this book. Jung was compelled by his own integrity to resuscitate the criticisms of Freud which he had suppressed, and once again, to trust his own independent judgement. If I were asked to sum up the difference between the two men in a single sentence I should point to the contrast in their fundamental values. Freud undoubtedly attributed supreme value to the orgastic release of sex, whereas Jung found supreme value in the unifying experience of religion. Hence Freud tended to interpret all numinous and emotionally significant experience as derived from, or substitutes for, sex : whereas Jung tended to interpret even sexuality itself as symbolic; possessing 'numinous' significance, in that it represented an irrational union of opposites, and was thus a symbol of wholeness.

The details of the break between the two, still differently reported by Freudians and Jungians, need not detain us here. It was foreshadowed in 1911, overt in 1912, and final in 1913. The effect upon Freud was to cause him considerable distress; and he later referred to Jung's departure as 'a great loss'. Jung always maintained that, after the blow of losing him, Freud's writing changed in character. The effect upon Jung, however, was more nearly shattering. In his autobiography, Jung refers to this period of his life as one of 'inner uncertainty' and 'a state of disorientation'. He also states that he lived 'under constant inner pressure' which was so strong that he suspected that there was 'some psychic disturbance' in himself. There was indeed. In the autumn of 1913 Jung reports that he felt as if the pressure within himself which was disturbing him was moving outwards, 'as though there were something in the air'. 'It was as though the sense of oppression no longer sprang exclusively from a psychic situation, but from concrete reality.' *In other words, Jung began to attribute an inner upheaval within his own mind to some disturbance in the external world.*

The next thing that happened was that Jung started to have visions of world-destruction, which, as every psychiatrist knows, are often the prelude to an acute schizophrenic episode. Jung himself decided that he was 'menaced by a psychosis'. His dreams and visions of world destruction continued throughout the early part of 1914. Then, on the 1st August of that year, the first World War broke out. Jung's reaction was surprising. He abandoned the idea that his dreams and visions were an indication that he himself was near a mental breakdown, and concluded that they were anticipations of the approaching world conflict, a theory which fitted aptly with his previous feeling that his sense of oppression sprang from concrete reality rather than from within himself. In spite of this, Jung considered that his most important task was to investigate his own dreams and visions. 'I had to try to understand what had happened and to what extent my own experience coincided with that of mankind in general. Therefore my first obligation was to probe the depths of my own psyche.'[3]

This apparently contradictory response can be understood if it is borne in mind that Jung looked upon himself, and other creative people, as being vessels through which superior or new insights were made manifest. As I pointed out above, this is how the young medium whom Jung studied also regarded herself; and interestingly enough, instead of thinking of her as an hysteric whose mediumship was evidence of mental instability, Jung refers to her as 'precociously matured'. She died at twenty-six, but when Jung saw her two years before her death, he says that he 'received a lasting impression of the independence and maturity of her personality'. Jung regarded creative persons, including himself, both as being 'ahead of their time', and also as being in touch with a source of superior wisdom which might be variously referred to as the 'collective unconscious' or later, quite openly, as God. If these premises are understood, it is comprehensible that Jung both regarded his own disturbance as an anticipation of the first World War and also that he considered it his duty further to explore his own psyche as a consequence. As a creative individual whose personal disturbance reflected whatever disturbance in the world had led to the catastrophe of war, understanding his own mental upheaval might lead to understanding the upheavals of the world itself. Throughout Jung's work there is an uneasy feeling that a confusion between 'inner' and 'outer' persists, especially in the later writings upon synchronicity. Such a confusion is evident in his own description of his progress through 1914 and subsequent years. In some passages, it appears that he admits being near a psychotic breakdown. In others, it seems that, although acknowledging a mental upheaval, he attributes this, not to disturbing factors within himself, but to events or to anticipation of events in the world outside.

At this point it is interesting to note that Jung often attempted to relate his patients' neuroses to the 'spirit of the age' rather than to more personal factors. It is, of course, reassuring if one is told that one's neurotic behaviour is in part the product of the times; and indeed this may to some extent be true. In the past, witches or other scapegoats were often blamed for what we should consider neurotic symptoms; and it is certainly arguable, as Jung maintained, that a lively religious faith protects an individual from neurosis. The point I want to make here is that Jung's interpretation of his own mental disturbance had repercussions upon the interpretations he gave to patients; and that one of these interpretations was that their mental disturbances might also be, if not evidence of superior insight, at least attributable to the state of the world or the Zeitgeist. One is irresistibly reminded of R. D. Laing's evaluation of schizophrenics as being people who possess superior wisdom but who are living in an insane society.

Jung of course recognized that his dreams, visions, and images were the same as those he encountered in schizophrenic patients. But he continued to regard himself as in a different category, as indeed he was, although perhaps not quite in the way which he himself envisaged. He wrote in his autobiography: 'It is, of course, ironical that I, a psychiatrist, should at almost every step of my experiment have run into the same psychic material which is the stuff of psychosis and is found in the insane. This is the fund of unconscious images which fatally confuse the mental patient. But it is also the matrix of a mythopœic imagination which has vanished from our rational age.'[4]

The borderline between being regarded as an inspired prophet or as mentally ill is often a narrow one. There is no doubt that Jung did regard himself in the former light, albeit humbly, as a vessel of inspiration rather than an originator of his insights. In 1950, when he was writing 'Answer to Job', he referred to the controversial nature of the book by calling it 'pure poison': but he added that he had to write it because he owed it to 'his people' to give them the benefit of this particular piece of insight. Another way of looking at these years of mental upheaval might be to say that Jung came near to having a schizophrenic breakdown, but did not succumb because he possessed an unusually strong ego, and because he was able to use his creativity as a defence against breakdown in the way in which other creative people, for example Strindberg, have also been able to do.[5] At all events the self-analysis which Jung was forced to pursue during 1914–18 shaped the whole course of his subsequent psychological theorizing, and

also profoundly influenced his technique of psychotherapy. It was during these years that he discovered the
technique of 'active imagination', that he learned to
value painting as a method of objectifying phantasies,
and that he came to attach such enormous importance
to mandala symbolism. As he wrote himself : 'The years
when I was pursuing my inner images were the most
important in my life – in them everything essential was
decided. It all began then; the later details are only
supplements and clarifications of the material that burst
forth from the unconscious, and at first swamped it. It
was the *prima materia* for a life's work.'[6]

In 1913 Jung attained the age of 38. The mental upheaval through which he passed would now be described
as a 'mid-life crisis'. Elliott Jaques, in his excellent paper
on the subject,[7] has drawn attention to the frequency
with which creative persons experience a profound
crisis at around this age, which often results in a change
in outlook, and, after an interval, a difference in the
quality of the work produced. Professor Jaques also
notes that the death rate amongst creative artists shows
a sudden peak in the late thirties, and quotes Mozart,
Raphael, Chopin, Rimbaud, Purcell, Baudelaire, and
Watteau as examples. Jung's mid-life crisis was of psychotic intensity and he writes that he retained his grip
on reality only because he was anchored to the external
world by his wife and five children and by the needs of
his patients. In 1909 he had given up his appointment at
the Burghölzli hospital. In the midst of his crisis, he gave
up his lectureship at the University of Zürich, feeling
that he could no longer lecture until he had succeeded in
formulating the new orientation which was taking shape
within him. From this point on, Jung was entirely on his
own, and was little influenced by the ideas of others. As
a result he was successful in producing a vast body of
written material enshrining a point of view which in-

deed is highly original. The further details of his life need not concern us, since it was externally uneventful. Jung continued to live and practise in Küsnacht, Zürich, until his death in 1961, interspersing his routine with various trips abroad which are recorded in his autobiography. The foundations of his thought had been laid in childhood and youth. The crisis through which he passed in the war years forced him to recognize and come to terms with his own uniqueness as a creative person. The rest of his life was devoted to the elaboration of the insights which he attained during his self-analysis, and to their therapeutic extension from the solution of his own problems to the solution of the problems of others.

Having outlined the personal bases upon which Jung's thinking rested, it is possible to examine his contributions in rather more detail. In accordance with his need, already mentioned, to reconcile 'objective' and 'subjective', his early work at the Burghölzli hospital can be seen as falling into two parts. The first and more 'objective' is based upon the use of word-association tests. In the nineteenth century, many thinkers attempted to explain mental functioning in terms of association; that is, by studying the way in which mental contents are linked together by similarity, contrast, or contiguity in space and time. Associationist theories laid the foundation for Pavlov's idea of conditioning, which essentially depends upon one stimulus being associated with another. The bell which has been associated with food on a number of occasions will produce salivation as if it were food, even when the latter is omitted. Word-association tests use a list of words as stimuli to which the subject is required to respond by saying the first word which occurs to him in response to the stimulus word. It is usual to read out a list of about a hundred words, and to time the interval between stimulus and response by means of a stopwatch. Word-association tests have been used for a number of purposes. It was originally hoped that they might throw light upon the differences between various types of intelligence. Instead, they became useful tools for detecting emotional preoccupations.

When a stimulus word is read out, the subject will respond rapidly with a 'reaction word' to all stimulus words which are emotionally indifferent to him. But, if the stimulus word carries an emotional significance, the subject will hesitate, fail to respond, make mistakes, stammer, make involuntary movements, or show other evidence of disturbance. The commonest indicator of such disturbance is simply a prolongation of the 'reaction time'; that is, the interval between reading out the stimulus word and the production of a reaction word in response. Many subjects are quite unaware of (unconscious of) this delay in their response to significant words. Hence the test not only gives some hints as to what the emotional preoccupations of a subject may be, but also provides a striking demonstration of the fact that a person can be unconscious of what is significant to him. The test is therefore good evidence of the existence of some such mechanism as the Freudian notion of repression; since it demonstrates that emotionally-disturbing material can be banished from consciousness. Jung gives as an example of what the test can reveal the case of a man who showed disturbance in his responses to five words: *knife, lance, beat, pointed,* and *bottle*. Jung deduced that he had had a fight when drunk, taxed the man with it, and discovered that he had indeed spent a year in prison as a result of a brawl in which he had knifed someone. The subject was quite unaware of the fact that he had hesitated in response to the critical words.

Jung also demonstrated that, between certain members of a family, notably between mother and daughter, or sometimes between husband and wife, there might be such close links that a large number of their responses to stimulus words were identical. This was not, in Jung's view, a healthy state of affairs, since it indicated that one or both of the parties concerned had failed to attain sufficient individuality. Jung was always very well aware of the danger of mental contagion; of the adverse effect that one personality might have upon another. Instead of using the more familiar psychoanalytic term 'identification', he generally refers to 'contagion' or 'participation mystique'. Jung believed that, when two people were intimately associated, a peculiar, unconscious association took place which might have harmful effects. This was a danger to which analysts, because of the nature of their work, were particularly susceptible. On the other hand, he also believed that it was impossible to help a patient unless the analyst was to some extent affected by him. Speaking informally, Jung once said: 'Your unconscious runs away with the patient's unconscious.' He also referred to analysts 'going queer'; and went on to say that he thought Freud had been adversely affected by his patients. This emphasis upon too close an association between minds as being dangerous is interesting in view of the later development of Jung's psychology, with its emphasis upon 'individuation'; the individual becoming himself, a unique person, emancipated from undue influence, and, indeed, almost exclusively concerned with his own inner development. It is also a point of view more likely to occur to a psychiatrist working with psychotics rather than neurotics. Anyone who has practised psychotherapy with psychotics will confirm that delusional systems, and other features of the psychotic's world, are indeed contagious and may have a very disturbing effect upon the mind of the therapist.

It was as a result of his work with word-association tests that Jung introduced the term 'complex' into psychology. A complex is a collection of associations linked together by the same feeling-tone, as in the instance of the words and their associations given above. When complexes are touched upon, the person concerned shows evidence of emotional disturbance; and Jung demonstrated this disturbance not only by measuring the prolonged reaction-time to stimulus words, but by recording the subject's depth of respiration, the electrical resistance of his skin, and his pulse-rate. These physiological indicators alter in response to emotion. Jung was thus one of the first experimentalists to demonstrate the dynamic effects of forgotten, 'repressed' mental contents. The word 'complex' is now seldom used; and most people associate the word with a kind of loose talk of 'having complexes' fashionable in the nineteen-twenties and thirties, when psychoanalysis first entered the vocabulary of the sophisticated. For Jung, the concept was important, not only because the experimental demonstration of unconscious complexes supported Freud's theory of repression, but also because it bore out his own notion of the mind as divided into partial personalities. It is characteristic of Jung that, having demonstrated the existence of complexes, he should then begin to personify them. In his Tavistock Lectures of 1935 Jung refers to a complex as having 'the tendency to form a little personality of itself. It has a sort of body, a certain amount of its own physiology. It can upset the stomach. It upsets the breathing, it disturbs the heart – in short, it behaves like a partial personality.' Later he goes on to say: 'I hold that our personal unconscious, as well as the collective unconscious, consists of an indefinite, because unknown, number of complexes or fragmentary personalities.'[1] He even refers to complexes as possessing will-power and a kind of ego. As a child, he thought of both his mother and himself as possessing at least two personalities. Now, in studying patients, he came to the conclusion that everyone had many personalities. It is clear that Jung was impatient with the conventional diagnostic categories of psychiatry; and it appears that, for him, there was a continuum existing between 'normal', 'hysterical', and 'schizophrenic'. In his view, all human beings were divided selves. The difference between neurotic dissociation and schizophrenic dissociation lay in the fact that the latter was more profound and far-reaching. Jung perceived that, in schizophrenia, the patient's ideas and concepts lost cohesion both associatively, within the mind, and also with the environment in a way which did not occur in a merely neurotic disturbance. Indeed, for many years Jung did not think that schizophrenic fragmentation and dissociation could be the result of purely psychogenic factors, and postulated a hypothetical 'metabolic toxin', something like the drug mescaline, to account for the profundity of the psychic cleavage. As late as 1958, Jung was cautious enough to allege no more than that he thought that a psychogenic cause for schizophrenia was 'more probable' than a toxic cause. However, in spite of his original belief in an organic, physical cause for the disease, Jung did not hesitate to investigate the psychological meaning and significance of schizophrenic delusions, hallucinations and visions in a way which had never been done before. The result of his interpretations were published in 'The Psychology of Dementia Praecox' which first appeared in 1906. Jung sent the book to Freud, and it was this which led to Freud's invitation to Jung to visit him in Vienna in 1907.

This book is of historic interest, as it represents the first coherent attempt to apply psychoanalytic understanding to insanity. Jung demonstrated that, just as apparently senseless neurotic obsessions and phobias had a meaning, so also did the more fragmentary and incoherent utterances and beliefs of the insane. This search for meaning in the apparently incomprehensible may be said to represent the other aspect of Jung's mental hospital work; the 'subjective', as opposed to the 'objective' activity of giving association tests, measuring reaction-times and the like. One example which Jung quotes more than once is of the chronic schizophrenic patient who had been for almost fifty years in hospital who made stereotyped movements with her hands and arms. These movements resembled those made by village cobblers when sewing shoes. Upon the patient's death her elder brother told Jung that she had been in love with a shoemaker who had rejected her just before she became mentally ill. The movements were those of her lover, and indicated her close identification with him.

Reading through Jung's account of the cases he cared for in the Burghölzli impresses one with the thoroughness and persistence with which he studied and interpreted psychotic phantasies. It is often forgotten that Jung was a pioneer in the psychotherapy of the psychoses, a task which requires enormous stamina. He was proud of his own strength in this connection; and when, on one occasion, an American therapist who spent up to sixteen hours a day with a single patient was discussed with him, said, 'Ah, I was like that once!' It must have been an exciting period in which to begin a psychiatric career, for Freud's ideas promised a new approach to the understanding of mental disorder, and everyone at the Burghölzli was studying them, and attempting to prove or disprove them. Jung soon came to realize that psychotic phantasies were very similar to dreams, and he was able to understand at least some of them by applying the principles of dream-analysis which Freud had laid down in 'The Interpretation of Dreams'. But he fairly soon concluded that, although Freud's ideas fitted hysteria very well in many cases, they were less satisfactory when applied to schizophrenia. Although it was often possible to take the content of a delusional system and to trace its origin to infantile sexuality, as Freud had done in the case of the paranoiac Schreber, this procedure seemed to do less than justice to the creative complexity of the delusional material which might resemble a novel, a poem, or, more especially, a myth or fairy story. Interestingly enough, Freud came close to Jung's point of view when he wrote in his paper on Schreber: '*The delusional formation, which we take to be the pathological product, is in reality an attempt at recovery, a process of reconstruction.*'[2] This paper of Freud's was written before the break with Jung; and in it he refers to Jung's 'extraordinary analytic acumen'; but although world-reconstruction phantasies are recognized by psychoanalysis as occurring in schizophrenia, Freud seems to have made little subsequent use of the notion. Had he done so, it is probable that one of the most unsatisfactory parts of psychoanalytic theory would have been modified: Freud's views on creativity and artistic production. Freud never really grasped the notion that art might be a way of enhancing man's grip on reality rather than escaping from it into wish-fulfilling phantasy. For Freud, the reductive approach of tracing psychological material to its infantile origin always took precedence over the possibility that the same material might contain within it the seeds of a better adaptation and thus be forward-looking. Jung very early emphasized the positive and prospective nature of delusional systems. In a lecture delivered in 1914 he wrote: 'Closer study of Schreber's or any similar case will show that these patients are consumed by a desire to create a new world-system, or what we call a *Weltanschauung*, often of the most bizarre kind. Their aim is obviously to create a system that will enable them to assimilate unknown psychic phenomena and so adapt themselves to their own world. This is a purely subjective adaptation at first, but it is a necessary transition stage on the way to adapting the personality to the world in general.'[3]

Once again, we meet Jung's preoccupation with the problem of reconciling the subjective with the objective; how to connect the delusional system which expresses the patient's subjective myth with the objective reality of the external world. This preoccupation had a consequence which, at first, looks curious, but which is actually important in understanding Jung's later work. This consequence was to bring what is usually considered 'normal', and what is usually considered 'psychotic' closer together. Jung's appraisal of delusional systems as subjective myths which happened to be at variance with the external reality of the world led him to make comparison of psychotic delusions and phantasies with the myths and religious systems of other peoples and other historical periods. He found many similarities. Although Jung did not put it in quite these words, it is obvious that he came to consider myth as 'adaptive' (to use modern biological terminology). Just as schizophrenics were attempting to create a world system which enabled them 'to assimilate unknown psychic phenomena and so adapt themselves to their own world' so the myths of primitive people were devices enabling them better to adapt to *their* world.

As an example of what Jung meant, one might quote from his visit to the Pueblo Indians of New Mexico. These people believe (or, as Jung might have put it 'live by the myth' that) the sun is their father. Moreover, they also affirm that, by practising the rites of their religion, they assist the sun to perform his daily journey across the sky. By punctiliously performing these rites, they are thus benefiting the whole world; and, if they were foolish enough to neglect them, 'in ten years the sun would no longer rise. Then', Jung's informant went on, 'it would be night for ever.' Jung's comment on this is as follows : 'I then realized on what the "dignity", the tranquil composure of the individual Indian, was founded. It springs from his being a son of the sun; his life is cosmologically meaningful, for he helps the father and preserver of all life in his daily rise and descent.'[4] If a myth can give life dignity, meaning, and purpose, it is serving an important positive function, *even if it is not objectively true.* Although, quite obviously, the delusions of schizophrenics were myths that did not work, in that the schizophrenic had to live in hospital and not in the community of ordinary persons, yet it might be that delusional systems were abortive efforts at finding new adaptations; and there was no reason to dismiss them as merely silly, just because they were not 'true' in the conventional sense. After all, Jung argued, thousands of normal Christians believed in the Virgin Birth; and this also was a myth which could not possibly be 'true' in any scientific sense. Yet, not all Christians were mad. Moreover, Jung knew from his studies in comparative religion that the theme of the virgin birth of a saviour or hero was not confined to Christianity. It is this way of looking at psychological phenomena which led to Jung's making such remarks as 'An idea is psychologically true inasmuch as it exists.'

Thus, 'normal' and 'mad' or schizophrenic were relative terms, not absolutes; and so-called normal men also had myths by which they lived, which were not objectively true. Perhaps myths were a necessary adaptive mechanism which promoted health, and perhaps the fact that so many modern men appeared neurotic and unhappy was because they had somehow become alienated from the myth-creating substratum of the mind which was shared both by the normal person and by the psychotic.

Of course the weak point in this comparison is that it fails to distinguish adequately between psychotic and normal. If schizophrenic delusional systems are not really much different from religious beliefs which serve a positive adaptive function, why is it that schizophrenics are so poorly adapted to the world that they have to live in hospital? Jung never really answers this question; but it is fair to say that no one else has done so fully satisfactorily. Cross-cultural studies reveal that something like 'schizophrenia' exists in most cultures; and of course it is obvious that what a Western psychiatrist might consider a delusion in a Western patient would be wrongly so regarded if it occurred in a man from a primitive Nigerian village. In Western culture, the presence or absence of 'delusions' is one of the diagnostic criteria of schizophrenia. These criteria are overdue for revision. Although certain 'delusions', for instance, those of being poisoned, or of having thoughts put into one's head by someone else, are rather typical of schizophrenia, the presence or absence of many other mental contents which most psychiatrists are apt to dismiss as delusional is a poor criterion of mental disease. Are we to dismiss all Christian scientists, theosophists, spiritualists, believers in astrology or flying saucers, as schizophrenic? What we need is a diagnostic criterion based, not upon the presence or absence of delusions, but upon the patient's failure to adapt to the external world, the weakness of his ego, and the liability of his mind to show 'splitting'; the fragmentation already mentioned as characteristic. Although Jung did not provide us with a new set of diagnostic criteria, his recognition of the fact that schizophrenic delusional systems are not really very different from many of the beliefs held by normal people is important and not generally appreciated. Indeed, it might be said that Jung came to the conclusion that everyone possesses his own 'delusional system', although he did not use this terminology. He would rather have said that every man needs a myth by which to live, and that if he does not appear to possess one, he is either unconscious of it, or else sadly alienated from the roots of his being.

Amongst some of his schizophrenic patients, Jung came across examples of beliefs and ideas which were certainly bizarre, but which he recognized as being closely similar to beliefs and ideas held by persons in antiquity, or else by people from other cultures. One example was from a paranoid schizophrenic in hospital who one day took Jung to the window, pointed up at the sun, and told Jung that if he was to look at the sun with his eyes half-closed he would be able to see the phallus of the sun. If he were then to move his head from side to side, he would see that the sun's phallus moved too; and that was the origin of the wind. Some years later Jung came across a book by Albrecht Dieterich containing a Greek text thought to be a liturgy of the cult of Mithras, a deity with some rather close resemblances to Christ, who was originally worshipped by the Hindus and Persians, and who later became popular in Rome at the time of the Emperor Commodus. In reading this text, Jung came across a vision which exactly parallelled that of his patient. 'And likewise the so-called tube, the origin of the ministering wind. For you will see hanging down from the disc of the sun something that looks like a tube...'[5] The schizophrenic who told him of this vision was a clerk of no high degree of culture. Moreover, the book in which Jung later discovered the identical vision described had not been published at the time that the patient had been committed to hospital. It was possible, therefore, to be sure that the patient had not read the book, and also to be certain that Jung himself had not influenced the patient's thinking, since he himself was unaware of any such vision before the patient told him of it. Jung concluded that there was a myth-creating level of mind, common to both psychotics and normals, and common also to people of different times and different cultures. This level of mind he named the *collective unconscious.*

The example given is certainly a striking one; but it would be even more impressive if Jung had not made use of it quite so often. Throughout the Collected Works, it occurs over and over again. Moreover, Jung does not tell us whether he followed the patient's instructions and looked at the sun through half-closed eyes. As anyone pressing their eyeballs and looking at a bright light will testify, it is not difficult to create optical illusions in this way; and, as Freud averred in 'The Interpretation of Dreams', any long pointed object, even a ray of light, might take on a phallic significance. But it is certainly hard to account for the fact that both the liturgy and the patient entertained the idea that this solar phallus had something to do with the origin of the wind, except on the basis that minds remote from each other both culturally and in time have a tendency to produce similar images and ideas.

Jung has been much criticized for his concept of a collective unconscious; but I should be inclined to attribute this to the obscurity and confusion of his later writings upon the subject, rather than to any flaw in the idea itself in its pristine and simplest form. In fact, it seems intrinsically likely that whatever parts of the mind may be considered responsible for producing dreams, visions, myths, and religious ideas should function rather similarly in different parts of the world and at different periods. Man's basic anatomy and physiology has not altered much during the millenia of his existence. Nor, in essentials, have many of his basic psychological experiences. Myths are both expressive of these experiences, and also attempt to provide explanations of the world in which man finds himself. The hero myths, for example, which have been extensively studied by Jung and his followers, show striking similarities from whatever culture they may come. The hero who, often originating in obscurity, receives the call to adventure, leaves home, faces dangers, slays a dragon or other monster, and is finally rewarded for his bravery by a throne and a beautiful bride, is familiar to most people from the myths and fairy stories which they read in childhood. It is not difficult to see that such myths express one set of fundamental psychological experiences common to all men. We all start life as helpless children. We all have to emancipate ourselves from parents and other adults and face life and its challenges independently. If we do not succeed in doing so, we will neither attain a position in the world (a throne), nor reach sufficient heterosexual maturity to win a mate (the beautiful princess). Instead, we shall be destroyed by the dragon; and everyone must surely be familiar with at least one family in which a son has been destroyed by a dragon of a mother from whom he has been unable to emancipate himself, even if it was he who made her into one by his failure to seek freedom. Hero myths originating from different cultures are similar because our psychological progress through life is similar, whether we were reared in New York, or belong to the Netsilik Eskimos; whether we live in the twentieth century or the fifth century before Christ.

Hero myths can be regarded as expository rather than explanatory. They give shape, form, and often artistic expression to emotional experience. Other myths, like those of the creation of the world, are explanatory rather than expository. They are like a primitive form of science, purporting to account for the facts of the world as they appear to pre-scientific man. Both forms of myth tend to order experience, to make it more coherent. If Jung had expounded his hypothesis of the collective unconscious in terms of man's need for art and for science, instead of in terms of his need for religion, I believe the idea would have become far more widely acknowledged. Jung, however, was severely hampered, not only by the fact that at the time when he was writing religious ideas were unfashionable, but by his own difficulty in expressing his thoughts with clarity. I know of no creative person who was more hamstrung by his inability to write.

However, it seems probable that the time which he spent at the Burghölzli laid the foundation for a good many of the ideas which later became keystones of Jungian thought. First, there was experimental confirmation for his notion that the mind was, or could be, divided into differing parts which he tended to personify. Second, the idea occurred to him that there was a substratum of mind common to all men which was the source of mythological, cosmogonic notions. Third, he conceived that this mythological material had a positive function in giving meaning and significance to man's existence; perhaps as a compensation for his actual insignificance, just as the grandiose delusions of schizophrenics compensated for their failure in life. Fourth was the idea that such material was not only compensatory, but prospective; that is, forward-looking in its application. A myth might be an attempt on the part of the mind itself at self-healing; that is, at creating a better adaptation in the future. Fifth, this point of view implied that not all dreams, phantasies and similar material could be interpreted in terms of the subject's infantile past, as Freud would have it. Nor could it be maintained that the creative energy of the mind – the libido – was wholly sexual. Whilst hysterical neuroses were generally connected with a sexual disturbance, schizophrenia was concerned with a more general failure in adaption to external reality. The connection between the inner world of the subject and his whole view of the external world could not be thought of as merely a sexual phenomenon.

3 Archetypes and the Collective Unconscious

The word 'archetype' has passed into more or less general use; but it is extraordinarily hard to give an adequate definition of the term as used by Jung. In the last chapter, I drew attention to Jung's conception of a 'collective unconscious' responsible for the spontaneous production of myths, visions, religious ideas, and certain varieties of dream which were common to various cultures and periods of history. I instanced the so-called hero myths as illustrating what was meant; and pointed out that such a myth could be held to be an exposition, in fairy-tale language, of a child's progress from infancy to maturity. Although the basic essentials of this progress are held in common by all mankind, since every child is born of a mother, has to grow up, attain independence, and win a mate, yet the details of such a progress will vary from culture to culture. Thus, the English would tend to portray the hero as controlled, courteous, reluctant to show emotion, honest, and straightforward; a 'gentleman' in fact, or a 'parfit gentil knyght'. A Greek hero, on the other hand, might be painted as being much cleverer; a trickster who would not shun deceit, would use guile to defeat his enemies, and who would not necessarily disdain displays of emotion when the situation warranted it. Odysseus is just as brave as any English Galahad; but Homer describes him as πολύτροπον – the man of many wiles. It is, therefore, as if there was some kind of flexible mould underlying the idea of the hero, which could not be clearly seen until a culture had filled it with a myth, and therefore to some extent rigidified it by defining it, but which itself was indefinable. When linguistic analysts study the relations between different languages, they not infrequently come across words from two or more languages which are so similar that they are bound to postulate a parent word from which each was clearly derived. Yet the parent language may be lost; so that the existence of the parent word is hypothetical. The archetype corresponds to the parent word, or to the flexible mould. It does not correspond to the actual manifestation as produced by any particular culture; yet it underlies all manifestations produced by all cultures. The nearest one can come to it is by parallel and comparison. *Das Ding an sich* – the thing in itself – will always escape precise definition. This, I think, is what Jung means when he writes: 'Again and again I encounter the mistaken notion that an archetype is determined in regard to its content, in other words that it is a kind of unconscious idea (if such an expression be permissible). It is necessary to point out once more that archetypes are not determined as regards their content, but only as regards their form, and then only to a very limited degree. A primordial image is determined as to its content only when it has become conscious and is therefore filled out with the material of conscious experience.'[1]

This formulation disposes of the accusation sometimes brought against Jung that he was a Lamarckian, believing in the inheritance of acquired characteristics. What is inherited is a predisposition, not an idea; a predisposition to create significant myths out of the common stuff of day-to-day human experience; just as one might say that a human being inherits a predisposition to react emotionally to the opposite sex. It is true that in other contexts Jung writes as if he did believe that culture affected these predispositions; more especially when he postulates racial differences in the collective unconscious: but these seem to be later accretions. The original idea that archetypes are inherited predispositions is no more Lamarckian than to say that the sexual instinct is inherited, or the structure of the cerebellum. Some confusion exists in that the word 'archetype', or the adjective 'archetypal' may refer to a situation, a figure or image, or to an idea of symbolic significance. Thus, when a hero meets a typical impasse, a ford which has to be crossed, a thick hedge which has to be pierced, a wall of fire which has to be penetrated, we are dealing with both an archetypal figure and an archetypal situation. Archetypes can also be equivalent to abstract ideas; the Christian Cross, for example, representing the death of the hero, on the one hand, and also an irrational union of opposites on the other.

Archetypes are felt to possess immense emotional significance. They are, if one likes to put it that way, typical human experience; but experience raised to what is felt to be of superhuman, or even cosmic significance. All human beings, at least in Jung's view, experience life archetypically, at least at times. Perhaps the easiest way of appreciating this is to take some typical human experience like sex. Sex can be the mere slaking of an 'all-too-human' appetite. (Jung is fond of phrases like 'all-too-human', and to a minor extent may merit the Freudian accusation of regarding sex *per se* as distasteful). On the other hand, sex can be experienced as transcendental love, a 'divine' afflatus, the most important thing in life. Anyone who has ever been passionately, head-over-heels in love will recognize the difference. Similarly, great plays raise the experience of the characters within them to a higher level than the merely personal. In the time of Shakespeare, one device for doing this was to make the characters 'royal'. The conflicts of a Prince of Denmark, a Cleopatra, or a King of England, however banal they may appear on critical analysis, are likely, on the stage, to take on a more than human, a mythic, an archetypal significance. Even more is this so in opera, where a very ordinary, and all too often confused story, becomes a vehicle for heroic passions, great events, and desperate tragedies, because the figures are transfigured and transmuted through the music, which lends them a significance they might not otherwise possess. It is not really surprising that Wagner, attempting the superhuman task of creating a completely new synthesis of poetry, music, and drama, should have been forced to turn to mythology (in the 'Ring') to lend his figures the timeless significance he needed. Indeed, as Robert Donington has demonstrated, the 'Ring' is a happy hunting-ground for Jungians.[2] In his autobiography, Jung, describing the progress of his own self-analysis, refers to archetypes as speaking 'the language of high rhetoric, even of bombast', a style which he found embarrassing. But, in the hands of a master like Shakespeare, because of his poetic gift, characters can speak in such language and enthral rather than embarrass us. Poetry, like music, can transmute the mud of the banal into the gold of the transcendent. One of Jung's central ideas was that modern man had become alienated from this mythopœic substratum of his being, and that therefore his life lacked meaning and significance for him. The task of analysis was to put him in touch once again with this absolute or 'divine ground', as Aldous Huxley would have called it, by means of analysing the subject's dreams. This point of view is perfectly coherent and sensible, provided one accepts the premise that what is wrong with neurotics is not primarily a disturbance in their sexual lives or a failure to make adequate personal relationships, but rather a loss of the sense that there is any meaning in existence. Modern 'existential' analysts are preoccupied with exactly the same problem; but seldom seem to recognize that Jung anticipated them.

The existence of the mythological substratum to human experience is recognized by analysts of entirely different theoretical orientation, though they would use another nomenclature. The 'object-relations' school of analysts refer to 'internal objects' which are presumed to be images of parents and other significant figures, derived from the infant's earliest experience, 'introjected', that is, enshrined within the psyche, and influencing all his subsequent experience of actual people in the external world. For example, let us suppose that an infant has been mishandled or neglected by his mother; and what mother is so perfect that she might never neglect or mishandle her infant? The baby will enshrine or introject a picture of the mother as a witch-like figure, a potential persecutor who is likely to damage him. On the other hand, when his mother is fulfilling all his needs, she will appear as a kind of protective goddess, a 'perfect' provider, comforter, and giver of love. Kleinian analysts write of the 'paranoid–schizoid' position as the earliest stage of emotional development of the infant; and the main feature of this stage is the separation of images of the mother into wholly 'good' and wholly 'bad'; images which can be personified as the Virgin Mary on the one hand, and an evil witch on the other. That these images exist as active factors in the human psyche is not in doubt. Anyone who has ever worked in a child guidance clinic will have had the experience of interviewing a child, hearing his description of his mother, and wondering what terrible figure will follow the child into the consulting room. When she actually appears, she is as likely as not to be a mild, kindly, ordinary sort of person, quite remote from the child's phantasy picture of her. On a collective scale, it is obvious that the same process of projecting images quite remote from reality occurred in the witch-hunts of the Middle Ages, when thousands of innocent old women were tortured and burnt because they were seen as evil persecutors. In Jungian terminology, such images are archetypal. They lie behind the child's actual experience of his actual parents. Put another way, one might say that these images represent the entirely subjective, and very primitive, needs and fears of the child, without much reference to external reality. These images tend to be reactivated in extreme situations. Thus, when men feel threatened by external events like the Black Death, they will regress to a primitive, 'paranoid–schizoid' stage of development, and seek for scapegoats whom they can blame for their predicament, whether these be the Jews, or anti-Christ, or witches. At the same time, they will call upon the Mother of God to save them, and will fall for the utterances of any leader who promises deliverance, seeing him as an idealized saviour without blemish. It is not difficult to prove the existence of an inner world of highly irrational images; and whether these are called archetypes or internal objects hardly seems to matter. Kleinian analysts would derive these images, at any rate for the most part, from the infant's actual experience; whereas Jung would have maintained that they were derived more from inborn predisposition in the manner outlined above. Interesting though this question may be theoretically, it is hardly relevant in practice. What does matter is how this inner world of internal objects or archetypal images is integrated into ordinary human existence. The Kleinian answer (and the Freudian, in so far as Freud recognized the 'inner world' problem) would presumably be that, in the ordinary course of emotional development, provided that the individual succeeds in making really satisfying emotional relationships with real people in the external world, the internalized images lose their emotional charge, and are only regressively reactivated under special circumstances; for instance, in disaster or bereavement. Jung, on the other hand, would have maintained that a place had to be found for the emotional charge attached to these images other than in interaction with the external world. Jung's answer to this is of course a religious one, although it is not an answer in terms of any particular variety of dogmatic creed or conventional system.

One difficulty which will occur to many people in this connection is as follows. We may accept the idea that it is only through myth that a man feels his life to have meaning and significance. Through the cold eyes of objectivity, no single individual matters very much. We are all insignificant atoms, not very different one from another, and most of us will be forgotten within a few years of our deaths. But if a man feels that he is assisting the sun in its daily transit, or that he is a child of God, or that he is destined for eternal life, or that he has a message for mankind, or that he is really a Prince, defrauded of his inheritance by the plots of Freemasons, then he is in a position to overcome his sense of his own futility. As will be perceived, I am putting forward suggestions as to possible myths which can be variously regarded either as paranoid delusions or as religious beliefs. As I pointed out in the last chapter, one weakness of the Jungian conception is that it fails to distinguish between psychotic and normal. I think that Kleinians and Freudians would argue that religious beliefs are as unnecessary as delusions, provided a man has sufficiently rewarding interpersonal relationships. After all, they might allege, where does the average person find his sense of his own worth? As a child, if he is loved sufficiently by his parents, he never questions the point of life or the meaning of his own existence; and he incorporates (introjects) so firm a sense of his own value because of what his parents have given him, that he continues throughout his life to feel significant. Moreover, when he marries, he will be sure of his value to his spouse, and later to his children. What is the need, in the normal person, for all this seeking after the significance of life, the meaning of existence? Surely it is only to the schizoid, alienated person that such questions occur. It is true that the infant starts life with an inner, subjective world which is at variance with the external objective world. But surely, in the normal person, the subjective and the objective intermingle sufficiently for there not to be too enormous a gap between them. We feel, and should feel, irrational about those we love; but out irrational inner world is sufficiently catered for by the irrational element in all emotional interpersonal relationships.

As we shall see, there is something in this charge. It may well be maintained that Jung was not only generalizing from his own experience, but also from the experience of a highly specialized group of patients to whom his point of view particularly appealed because of their likeness to himself. On the other hand, it may also be argued, as Jung did, that in practically every age except our own, man's need to find a home for his inner world in a religion was universally acknowledged; and that many people were suffering from a sense of futility just because they lacked a myth. Moreover, Jung would have pointed to the totally irrational belief in political systems, be it Communism or Fascism or National Socialism, as greatly inferior forms of religious belief which took hold of men's minds, willy-nilly, just because they had discarded the beliefs of their ancestors which were actually far more 'reasonable'. It is more sensible, and probably less likely to do harm to other people, if one worships God rather than Mao-Tse Tung or the State in spite of the Inquisition and the wars of religion. The need to worship something or somebody is, however, not to be extirpated; or, if it is, leaves a man with a sense of futility and a consequent liability to fall for all kinds of totally absurd beliefs, whether these be political, or such phantasies as spiritualism, astrology, theosophy, and the like.

This is a book about Jung, and not about the ideas of the present author; but I cannot avoid mentioning, at this juncture, that I think Jung was right in supposing that interpersonal relationships cannot contain the whole of man's inner world. In another book I have argued that man's infancy is intrinsically frustrating; and that it is this fact which makes him restlessly creative, searching for 'ideal' solutions, whether these be in the shape of scientific world-views, philosophies, religions, or the integrative patterns of art.[3]

We shall revert at a later point in this book to the more general effect of Jungian analysis and the attainment of what Jung called a religious attitude, albeit without subscribing to a generally accepted faith. At this point we must revert to a discussion of some of the more important archetypal figures themselves.

I hope I have made it clear above that Jung is perfectly justified in drawing attention to the fact that, in addition to the child's image and experience of his actual mother as a real person, one has to take into account 'archetypal' images of the good and bad mother which, as it were, become projected upon the real mother in such a way that she may appear as a kind of divinity or else as a kind of witch. In a paper on the mother archetype, Jung gives a list of ways in which this may manifest itself, ranging from mother goddesses to more abstract things which are associated with fertility, protection, containment, and the like. Since maternal protection (overprotection) can also be a threat to developing individuality, the negative aspects of the maternal archetype are expressed in such symbols as witches, dragons, devouring and entwining animals and situations, and even the grave, or the sea in which the individual may drown.

As I pointed out in the first chapter, the father plays a much smaller part in Jungian psychology than in Freudian (compare the entries under 'mother' with those under 'father' in the index of 'Symbols of Transformation'). But the father also has his archetypal aspects. As in the case of the mother, the image has opposite faces. On the one hand, the archetypal father is 'the representative of the spirit, whose function it is to oppose pure instinctuality';[4] a sublime deity, 'the symbol of the most complete sexual repression'.[5] On the other, he is the devil, 'the symbol of sexual lust'.[6] In an early paper 'The Father in the Destiny of the Individual' written when Jung was still under the influence of Freud, though later considerably revised, Jung comes close to what might now be considered a Kleinian point of view. He writes that 'The parental influence, dating from the early infantile period, is repressed and sinks into the unconscious, but is not eliminated; by invisible threads it directs the apparently individual workings of the maturing mind. Like everything that has fallen into the unconscious, the infantile situation still sends up dim, premonitory feelings, feelings of being secretly guided by other worldly influences. Normally these feelings are not referred back to the father, but to a positive or negative deity'.[7] In this passage, Jung appears to consider that the archetypal images take origin from infantile experience, rather than being based upon inherited predispositions. If Jung had continued to maintain this point of view about the origin of archetypal images, he would have gained wider acceptance for his psychology.

The disagreement as to the origin of 'internal objects' or archetypes is mirrored by the disagreement between biologists as to what is learned and what is innate. Not all adaptive behaviour is the result of learned experience. There are inherited predispositions, probably imbedded in the structure of the nervous system, which incline animals to behave in certain ways. One example is of the male salticid spider. In approaching a female, he has to perform a specific ritual courtship dance in such a way that the female responds in a sexual way. If he performed his dance in any other way, she would immediately eat him. But he has no opportunity in his short life to gain any information about what a female of his own species looks like, nor what movements he must perform to inhibit her feeding reactions and to stimulate her specific mating responses.[8] Therefore his performance of his dance must be a behaviour pattern which is largely innate.

It seems highly probable, though difficult to prove, that the human infant is born with a number of innate predispositions to which to respond; for example, parents, the opposite sex, and rather basic human situations like having children, separating from parents in adolescence, and finally, death. These innate predispositions might be compared to the 'innate releasing mechanisms' (IRMs) described by Tinbergen in animals. Many animals have a built-in tendency to respond in a fairly stereotyped way to certain specific stimuli in the environment. Jung comes close to this when he writes: 'There is no human experience, nor would experience be possible at all, without the intervention of a subjective aptitude. What is this subjective aptitude? Ultimately it consists in an innate psychic structure which allows man to have experiences of this kind. Thus the whole nature of man presupposes woman, both physically and spiritually. His system is tuned in to woman from the start, just as it is prepared for a quite definite world where there is water, light, air, salt, carbohydrates, etc. The form of the world into which he is born is already inborn in him as virtual images, as psychic aptitudes. These *a priori* categories have by nature a collective character; they are images of parents, wife, and children in general, and are not individual predestinations.'⁹

What Jung claims to have done is to have isolated these images from individual experience by his technique of comparing myths from differing cultures. Although an archetype may be ultimately indefinable in itself, one can get some idea of it if one accumulates enough different manifestations of it cross-culturally and in different periods of history. This accounts for one difficulty with which the reader is faced in tackling the Collected Works of Jung. Jung has a tendency to pile parallel upon parallel from his very extensive knowledge of myth and comparative religion in such a way that the reader may easily forget what it was that was originally being discussed.

There is no theoretical limit to the number of archetypes; but, in practice, some are more important than others. I have already discussed the archetypal images underlying the child's experience of his actual parents. Just as important as these are the archetypal images underlying a person's experience of the opposite sex. Jung names these images *animus* and *anima*; the former term referring to a woman's image of a man, and the latter to a man's image of a woman. In Jung's writings, the anima plays a more prominent role than the animus, presumably because as a man he found the female image more easily definable. Perhaps the simplest way of approaching the concept is by way of the common human experience of falling in love. When a man becomes passionately infatuated with a commonplace girl, his friends may say to each other 'What on earth does he see in her?' What he sees is, in Jungian terminology, the anima. At one level, the anima is simply a personification of male erotic desire; an image which may become projected upon a real woman, but which may have little to do with the actual nature of the real person. The anima is described not only as being erotically seductive,

but as possessing age-old wisdom; an attribute which at
first sight may seem incongruous. Why should wisdom
be associated with erotic fascination? One of Jung's
favourite illustrations from fiction of what he meant by
the anima is Rider Haggard's 'She'. 'She', it will be remembered, is not only spectacularly beautiful, but also
an immortal priestess, with access to arcane knowledge
and a serene grasp of the esoteric. This idea is not as
remote from ordinary experience as may at first appear.
If a man is somewhat alienated from emotion and instinct – a common characteristic of schizoid intellectuals
– the woman who fascinates him erotically, and leads
him back into the human fold by teaching him the 'wisdom of the body' will appear to him to possess a
superior, age-old insight. There is a good example to be
found in Hermann Hesse's 'Steppenwolf', a character
who might be described as the archetype of the alienated
man. A quite ordinary young woman who takes pity on
his isolation, and seduces him, becomes his initiator into
a fantastic psychological progress which ends with his
confronting himself as he actually is. (The novels of
Hermann Hesse are another example of a happy hunting-
ground for Jungians.)

The anima is also described as being a link between
conscious and unconscious, or even, on occasion, as a
personification of the unconscious. (One of the major ob-
stacles in reading Jung is his multiplicity of ill-formu-
lated definitions for the same thing.) I think this notion
of the anima is best grasped by stating that erotic experience can 'open the door' to a world of feeling and emotion which is not necessarily or wholly erotic. We recognize that the person who has never been in love lacks not
only experience of the erotic, but also a whole dimen-
sion of human understanding. It is through their experience of the erotic that most people become
acquainted with 'passion' and the value attaching to

emotion. It is for this reason that, for many people, the erotic relation appears to contain 'the meaning of life' itself.

The animus, woman's image of man, is less easily defined, partly, as I have said, because Jung himself was a man and partly because, according to his account, the animus manifests itself as a multiplicity of male figures rather than a single one. 'Whereas the man has, floating before him, in clear outlines the significant form of a Circe or a Calypso, the animus is better expressed as a bevy of Flying Dutchmen or unknown wanderers from over the sea, never quite clearly grasped, protean, given to persistent and violent motion. These expressions appear especially in dreams, though in concrete reality they can be famous tenors, boxing champions, or great men in faraway, unknown cities.'[10] Ibsen, in 'The Lady from the Sea', has painted a picture of a woman who is unable to make a proper relation with her husband because of an ancient infatuation with a mysterious Stranger, a mariner whom she had briefly encountered on board ship and who then disappeared. The infatuation was consecrated by the couple throwing their rings into the sea – a kind of mystical marriage, Mysterium Conjunctionis, as Jung would have called it. The Stranger is a picture of what Jung meant by the animus, or at least one aspect of the figure; and one cannot do better than read 'The Lady from the Sea' if one wants to grasp the notion. At the end of the play, the Stranger himself reappears, and Ellida, the wife, has to choose between her husband and this 'demon lover'; a confrontation not unlike that required by Jung of his patients in analysis. According to Jung, it is only when a man or woman understands, becomes familiar with, and faces these personifications of subjective desire and emotion that they cease to operate as autonomous personalities, in opposition to the conscious will. Jung describes how, in his own self-analysis, he conducted long conversations with the anima. He also says that, once he had really understood the contents of the unconscious, he no longer needed the anima as intermediary – in other words, that he became more directly in touch with his own inner world of emotion, although he does not put it quite so simply. When Ellida confronts the Stranger, he loses his magical power over her, and she is able to choose to live with, and to love, her own husband in a way which she could not, so long as her phantasy infatuation had her in its grip. Another example of a typical animus figure is Mr Rochester in 'Jane Eyre'. Because he has a secret – his mad wife – and because he is in a superior social position, he appears to Jane as a mysterious figure, who is also dominant and ruthless. We are not told whether, after Jane married him, he continued, in her eyes, to display these attractive qualities. For the animus or anima to be fully projected requires that the recipient of the projection be somewhat remote. Greta Garbo, who of all film stars provided the most apt frame upon which to project anima images, is a case in point. Perhaps deliberately, perhaps because to do so reflected her real nature, she kept herself inaccessible. A close knowledge of Garbo as a real person would have destroyed the possibility of projecting so much upon her.

The anima and animus, then, are personifications of parts of the personality which are in some senses opposed to the conscious ego, and possess certain attributes of the opposite sex. Jung writes of the anima as causing moods, and the animus as producing opinions. By this he means that a man in the grip of emotion tends to become moody, sentimental, and childish, whereas a woman becomes argumentative, irritable, and opinionated.

Jung, true to his generation, believed that the sexes were strongly differentiated psychologically as well as physically. He would have had little sympathy with 'unisex' or women's liberation; and a recurrent theme throughout his writing is the disastrous effect which he thought universities – especially American universities – had upon the personality of women. He called them 'animus incubators'; by which pejorative phrase he indicated his belief that universities were apt to turn women into inferior imitations of men, making them competitive, argumentative, and full of ideas which they had taken over from men, but never properly grasped. Indeed, the animus, unlike the anima, comes off rather badly in Jung's descriptive writing. Of course, both figures have negative as well as positive aspects. A man 'possessed by the anima' is not a proper man. He is soft, emotional, moody, over-sensitive; not at all what a man should be in Jung's conception. And if this identification with the feminine, or failure to identify with the masculine, went so far that the man was homosexual, Jung did not approve at all. He was notoriously intolerant of male homosexuals. In his writing, it is this negative aspect of the animus which is chiefly stressed. By that I mean that we hear a good deal of women who are identified with, or possessed by, the animus, and who therefore display the irritating characteristics already noted. But we hear rather little about the animus as a positive function relating the ego of the woman to her own unconscious, or putting her in touch with her feelings, as the anima of a man is supposed to do. It is important not to identify oneself with the anima, if one is a man, or with the animus, if one is a woman. Another way of putting this is to say that one should not, in Jung's view, allow emotion to gain the upper hand, or take over the function of the ego. A person possessed by, or overwhelmed by, emotion is not in the right relation to his own inner world. Indeed, Jung went so far as to allege that the primary disturbance in schizophrenia is a violent affect which disrupts the personality.[11]

Two points must occur to the critical reader who reflects upon Jung's writings on the animus/anima concept. The first is that, like Freud, Jung found it necessary to postulate an emotional part of the personality as opposed to a more rational part, but that instead of naming the emotional part the 'id' or some such name, his predilection for dividing the mind into separate 'personalities' which we have already noted, led him to adopt a terminology in which mental functions are treated as people. Second, Jung fails to make clear that his descriptions derive from, and are applicable to, human beings who are isolated or who have never achieved a satisfactory relation with the opposite sex. It is perfectly true that men unrelated to women, and women unrelated to men, tend to show some characteristics in their behaviour which might be thought of as belonging to the opposite sex. Women on their own often become rather managing, bossy, and opinionated. Men on their own display 'feminine' traits of fussiness, emotionality, and moodiness. It could be argued that such phenomena are a simple consequence of a lack of sexual satisfaction. If a person's immediate milieu contains no one of the opposite sex with whom to relate and upon whom to project their internal image, the lack of this relation may lead to the person trying to *be* what is missing in addition to being themselves. The 'natural state' for human beings is surely one in which the individual is in relation with the opposite sex, whether temporarily or permanently: and the lack of such relation must be expected to have some untoward consequences.

It could also be pointed out that persons who have not made adequate relationships with the opposite sex have often failed to do so because of early confusions about the roles of the sexes. It is generally recognized, for example, that to come of a family in which the mother 'wears the trousers' is apt to cause difficulty for children of both sexes. Jung, of course, was perfectly well aware of this; but chose to adopt a terminology which reflects only the ego's relation with 'internal objects' and says very little about actual relations between real human beings. The fact that our human relationships are distorted because we tend to project images upon the other person which derive from inside ourselves, whether these be from the past experience of parents or from other sources, is well recognized by analysts of every school. Analysis, in the practice of other schools, generally proceeds partly by examining the discrepancies between the actual person with whom the patient is in relation and his expectations of them as reflected in his projections. Thus, a man may be irritated with his wife because she differs from the image of his mother to which he hoped she would conform; or because she does not fit in with some other preconceived notion of woman as a seductress, as an inspiration, or even as a good cook. Analysts of other schools, however, do not generally encourage their patients to treat these preconceived notions as persons and to hold conversations with them. This procedure is clearly derived from that adopted by Jung in his own self-analysis.

One wonders what his relation to his own wife was like during this period. He says that the fact that he had a wife and five children kept him sane, as no doubt it did. But I think it could be argued that to distil the idea of the anima from one's own experience argues a considerable degree of emotional disconnection from persons in the environment. What I am suggesting is that the 'normal' person, happily related emotionally to a person of the opposite sex, will not generally be aware of any vast discrepancy between the object of his love, and the 'internal object' of erotic phantasy. Everyone has erotic phantasies; and everyone may be aware that there is some discrepancy between his phantasies and the persons to whom he is related in reality. The younger a person is, the more likely is this to be the case. The more isolated a person the more will his 'relationships' be with phantasy figures (the temptations of St. Anthony), and the more important will the latter be to him. The completely isolated man has only phantasy figures. It could be argued that the whole concept of the anima and animus arose from the fact that Jung was an emotionally isolated person, as he himself acknowledges in more than one passage. 'As a child I felt myself to be alone, and I am still, because I know things and must hint at things which others apparently know nothing of, and for the most part do not want to know. Loneliness does not come from having no people about one, but from being unable to communicate the things that seem important to oneself, or from holding certain views which others find inadmissible.'[12] This hypothesis about how Jung came to formulate his ideas does not, of course, imply that his formulations are wrong. Indeed, it is obvious that there are collective images of each sex, varying from epoch to epoch, and not corresponding in reality to any actual person, but liable to be projected upon public figures who happen to fit into a limited extent, in appearance if not in character, with whatever the Zeitgeist dictates as being ideally masculine or feminine. To discern such images clearly within oneself, however, requires an exceptional degree of detachment from human relationships and the external world; a kind of distillation of the subjective. In an earlier passage, I pointed out that extreme situations such as the plague, or, to take a more recent example, the collapse of the Weimar Republic, resuscitate images of idealized 'saviour' figures who can do no wrong, and wholly bad 'devil' figures who do nothing but evil. In stable conditions these images remain unconscious; but under threat of destruction or loss of all predictable security, human beings revert to a very early stage in their emotional development in which they both feel threatened by persecutors who are more powerful than they are, and at the same time need protectors who are, hopefully, more powerful than the persecutors. It seems likely that, to become fully cognizant of the anima or animus within oneself, a similar regression must also take place; a regression to that solipsistic, narcissistic stage of development which Freudians postulate as being the infant's condition before he has any real relation with objects in the external world at all. A person who remains in this condition, and who does not maintain contact with the external world is schizophrenic; but, as Jung demonstrated, and as some people report after experience with drugs like LSD, it is possible, though dangerous, to enter a psychotic state and then emerge from it again. In such a state, the images encountered are often but slenderly related to real persons. In 'The Varieties of Psychedelic Experience', the authors describe many subjects as encountering mythological figures and situations closely comparable with those described by Jung.[18]

Another archetypal figure to which Jung makes frequent reference is that of the 'shadow'. Jung postulates, with reason, that most human beings are not as virtuous as they appear, either to themselves or to others. We are all more grasping, licentious, greedy, envious – and so on, through all the deadly sins – than we like to think. This is a commonplace observation confirmed daily in the psychotherapist's consulting room. Where Jung differs from analysts of other schools is in claiming that this characteristic of human nature is both universal and personified. In dreams of Europeans, the shadow habitually appears as a figure of the same sex as the dreamer, but usually dark-skinned, 'devilish', or in some sense felt to be evil. Jung maintained that both Freudian and

Adlerian analysts were principally engaged with the 'shadow-side' of human nature; since they were concerned with exploring the primitive, selfish drives of sexuality on the one hand, and power on the other. It is certainly true that such a figure does sometimes appear in dreams. In one example known to the author, the dreamer encountered an Indian boy-prince for whom he felt intense loathing, but who insisted on embracing him, after which the figure disappeared. The dream might be taken as signifying the dreamer's attempt to come to terms with a homosexual component in himself, and also with other 'shadow' elements, ruthlessness, violence, and the like. But Jung is not at all clear in his discussion of how far the 'shadow' is really a collective figure, and how far personal. He writes: 'We are no longer aware that in carnival customs and the like there are remnants of a collective shadow figure which prove that the personal shadow is in part descended from a numinous collective figure.'[14] But what this collective figure might be is not clearly defined. The shadow is perhaps no more than a personification arising from the infantile tendency, already discussed, to divide persons into black and white categories; gods and devils, virgins and witches. This tendency is enshrined in creative productions of a rather unsophisticated kind like the old-fashioned Western or the detective stories of Conan Doyle. In works of this genre, the villains are wholly wicked, and the heroes impossibly virtuous; an incorruptible Sherlock Holmes confronts a Moriarty who is a 'Napoleon of crime'.

Rather similar criticisms may be brought to bear on Jung's concept of the 'wise old man'; an archetypal figure who appeared to him in his own self-analysis as Elijah, and later developed into the character called Philemon mentioned in the first chapter of this book. The wise old man represents 'the factor of intelligence and knowledge' or 'superior insight'. But it is not at all obvious, from Jung's account, in what way this figure differs from a father-figure, or even from an image of God. Moreover, it may be remembered that, at the age of twelve, Jung had already conceived the idea that there was a second personality within him, an old man of great authority. Everyone knows that, if one is faced with a problem or moral dilemma, there is a limit to what conscious thinking can achieve. A period of waiting, or 'sleeping on it', may well bring a solution which conscious striving failed to find; and in this way, illumination is felt by the subject to have come to him from a source beyond consciousness. The wise old man appears to be Jung's personification of this common human experience.

Before leaving the subject of archetypes, some reference must be made to the concept of the *persona*. This term is derived from the Latin for the mask assumed by actors, and is used by Jung to designate the role played by an individual in accordance with the expectations of society, as opposed to what the person is in reality. A man may become identified with his role, to the detriment of his personality. Thus, a judge may be always a judge, a doctor invariably a professional healer, or a minister may never lay aside his robes. It is a phenomenon frequently encountered in social life. In the sense that it is partly society which demands role-playing, the phenomenon of the persona may be labelled as a collective one. Society lays down how a judge should be, and how a minister of religion should behave. The persona is sometimes contrasted with the shadow, and sometimes with the animus or anima; which is simply a way of saying that those who are identified with their social role are generally those who are unaware of their own antisocial impulses, and out of touch with their own inner feelings. The most important archetype, the Self, will be discussed in a subsequent chapter on the individuation process.

In his description of archetypes and the collective unconscious, Jung may be said to have anticipated the point of view of those psychoanalysts who write in terms of an inner world of 'internal objects'. Jung may well be right in alleging that the characteristics of these figures are not directly derived from infantile experience, but are the result of inborn predisposition; the nature of man himself. More cross-cultural studies are needed which would critically compare, for example, the figures of the witch or the Magna Mater as they have appeared in the mythology of different peoples. The existence of an inner world of archetypal figures is not in doubt, although analysts would disagree as to its origin. Nor is the fact that, at least under special circumstances, behaviour is influenced by this inner world. In recent years, we have grown used to the assumption, borne out by animal studies, that the experiences of earliest infancy may have a permanent effect upon later adaptation. Many archetypal figures as described by Jung are closely similar to the figures of infantile phantasy, as analysts of other schools might name them. And there would be general agreement that it is under conditions of stress, whether induced by external disaster, or by internal emotional upheaval, that reason is overborne, and a person's conduct becomes governed by the dominants of his inner world. In trying to understand these phenomena, Jung's model is probably more fruitful for research than that of the Kleinians; since, by drawing attention to the similarities between the mythologies of different times and different cultures, Jung has provided a basis for comparative studies.

4 Psychological Types, and the Self-Regulating Psyche

There have been, throughout history, many attempts to classify human beings in terms of differences in temperament; and Jung pays ample tribute to his predecessors in his massive treatise on the subject, 'Psychological Types'. However, it was Jung who made 'extravert' and 'introvert' into household words, and, although his later subdivision of these two basic attitudes to life has not been generally accepted, extraversion and introversion continue to be regarded as useful concepts, and are used by Eysenck, for example, as basic 'dimensions of personality' in his experimentally-based classification. It will be remembered that, in his early work, Jung found certain similarities between hysteria and schizophrenia, in that splitting of the personality occurred in both disorders, though more profoundly in the latter. He later became more impressed with the differences between the two types of illness. He observed that hysterics invariably maintained contact with the external world, and some rapport with the psychiatrist. Schizophrenics, on the other hand, withdrew from the world around them, and were notoriously remote from human relationships. This difference was reflected in the phantasies produced by the two types of patients. In an early paper on the subject Jung notes that hysterical phantasies can always be accounted for in terms of the patient's antecedents and personal history, whereas, in schizophrenia, the phantasies are more like dreams, and also have an archaic and mythological quality.[1] I have already drawn attention to the fact that Jung found Freudian interpretations generally satisfactory when applied to hysteria, but insufficient when considering schizophrenic material. It is interesting that the paper from which these ideas are taken was delivered by Jung in 1913 in Munich. It was the last occasion on which he and Freud encountered each other. Jung goes on to describe what he calls a centrifugal movement of libido in hysteria, as contrasted with a centripetal movement in schizophrenia. By this he means that hysterics tend always to invest the outer world and its objects with emotional significance; whereas schizophrenics find meaning in the inner world and its objects (chiefly archetypes). At the same time as he was making these observations upon pathological cases, Jung became concerned to explain how it was that Freud and Adler could interpret neurosis so differently. In his own account of how he first became interested in psychological typology, Jung says that it was the differences between Freud and Adler which originally engaged his attention. I think that Jung's early observations upon hysteria and schizophrenia were equally important; and that, as we shall see, his later emphasis upon extraversion and introversion as 'normal' attitudes combined with his lack of interest in the developmental psychology of childhood led him to neglect the fact that the 'introverted' disorder of schizophrenia is evidence of more serious psychopathology than the 'extraverted' disorder of hysteria.

However this may be, Jung came to realize that Freud and Adler approached the same material from different points of view, and that a neurotic symptom, a dream, or indeed the structure of a personality, could be interpreted from either angle with apparently equal validity. In 'Two Essays on Analytical Psychology' Jung takes the case of a young woman suffering from anxiety attacks, and interprets her neurosis first from the Freudian point of view and then from the Adlerian. Her symptoms could either be seen as a manifestation of sexual repression and an unacknowledged Oedipal tie to the father, or else as a device for tyrannizing over her husband. The former interpretation acknowledges sexuality as the mainspring of the neurosis; the latter gives precedence to the desire for power. As Jung points out, which interpretation is preferred depends upon the psychology of the interpreter. Thus Freud and Adler must have different basic psychological attitudes, belong to differing 'psychological types'. In the Freudian scheme of things the object is all important; in the Adlerian, the subject always takes the first place. Jung writes: 'Certainly both investigators see the subject in relation to the object; but how differently this relation is seen! With Adler the emphasis is placed on a subject who, no matter what the object, seeks his own security and supremacy; with Freud the emphasis is placed wholly upon objects, which, according to their specific character, either promote or hinder the subject's desire for pleasure.'[2] In 'Psychological Types', Jung expands this latter statement, and at the same time, has a dig at Freudian theory. 'The Christian process of development encountered in Origen a type whose ultimate foundation was the relation to the object – a relation that has always symbolically expressed itself in sexuality and accounts for the fact that there are certain theories today which reduce all the essential psychic functions to sexuality too.'[3]

Later, Jung depicts introversion as being characterized by 'a hesitant, reflective, retiring nature that keeps itself to itself, shrinks from objects, is always slightly on the defensive and prefers to hide behind mistrustful scrutiny.' The extraverted attitude is, on the other hand, characterized by 'an outgoing, candid, and accommodating nature that adapts easily to a given situation, quickly forms attachments, and, setting aside any possible misgivings, will often venture forth with careless confidence into unknown situations. In the first case obviously the subject, and in the second, the object, is all-important."[4]

I have already mentioned that, because of his experience with schizophrenics, Jung could not accept Freud's conception that 'libido' – that is, psychic energy – was entirely sexual. Although hysterical symptoms could be explained in terms of the subject's failure to make an adequate erotic relation with objects, the schizophrenic's failure to make any proper relation with the external world at all could not be thus interpreted. If one were to do so, it would follow that the subject's only relation to reality was an erotic one, a theory which seemed intrinsically improbable. Thus Jung came to use the word 'libido' in a different sense from that in which Freud used it; as a synonym for psychic energy in general, an energy which could manifest itself as much in the 'will-to-power' of Adler as in the Eros of Freud. (It should be remembered that, at the historical period with which we are here concerned, Freud had not yet acknowledged the existence of any independent 'aggressive' drive in man, nor formulated his concept of the 'death instinct'. After his break with Freud, Jung seems never to have taken any further notice of psychoanalysis, which is a pity, as psychoanalysis changed a great deal, and many of Jung's ideas bear a close relation with those of Fairbairn and other psychoanalysts). In one passage, Jung refers to 'concupiscentia' and 'superbia', lust and pride, and relates these manifestations of the libido to the fundamental instincts of preservation of the species and self-preservation. These twin manifestations of instinct in man are clearly related to extraversion and introversion. In the sexual relation, the object is given a value so intense that a person in love, or a highly dependent individual, can be at the mercy of the object, losing all self-respect and pride in the process. Those who pursue power and total independence, on the other hand, undervalue their objects to the point at which they become incapable of love, since other people hardly count compared with the maintenance of their own superiority.

It might be said that extraverts tend to become over-involved with objects, and therefore run the risk of losing their own identities as separate persons. Introverts, in contrast, because of their insistence on preserving their separateness, are under-involved with objects, may lose contact with them altogether, and retreat into an ivory tower of emotional isolation.

There are persons who alternate between the two extremes, thus illustrating the fact that extraversion and introversion are to be thought of as mechanisms or habitual attitudes, not as fixedly determined characteristics which cannot be altered. Jung repeatedly states that, although he considered that the type to which a person belonged took origin from attitudes developed in early childhood, everyone shows evidence of making use of both mechanisms. Moreover, cases occur, so he alleges, in which there appears to be a radical alteration in attitude, so that a person who, for most of his life, has been a quiet, retiring introvert, may change into an outgoing, expansive extravert.

The concept of psychological types led to one of the most fruitful and valuable of Jung's ideas: that of self-regulation. From his consideration of Freud versus Adler, it was obvious that either point of view was one-sided, since each excluded the other. Yet both theories, as Jung ingeniously demonstrated, contained some elements of the truth. He came to the conclusion that what was not present in the conscious attitude could be discerned in the unconscious; and that the analysis of dream and phantasy revealed the extravert latent in the introvert, and vice versa. According to this idea, dreams, phantasies, and even neurotic symptoms, were compensatory, aiming at a better balance within the psyche.

It is obvious that some psychological material can be fruitfully regarded in this light. For example, a young woman had a dream in which she was being pursued by a steam-roller. As she reached the bottom of the garden and was about to be overwhelmed, her mother appeared on the other side of the fence and laughed with hideous glee at her predicament. The subject was extremely fond of her mother, who indeed had looked after her devotedly. As a child, the girl had suffered from a physical disability which had necessitated her having special feeding and a great deal of maternal 'overprotection'. This had actually kept her childish, and unduly dependent upon the mother. Hence, in the dream, the mother appears in a totally different light; as a menace, a destructive person who is 'steam-rollering' the subject's individuality out of existence, or at least acquiescing in her being crushed. The unconscious is compensating for the conscious adaption to the mother by demonstrating an entirely different aspect of the relationship. In more than one passage Jung refers to the well-known schizophrenic delusion that everyone knows his innermost thoughts. This, Jung alleges, is compensatory to the schizophrenic's emotional isolation. The man whom nobody knows conceives the notion that everyone knows all about him.

The perceptive reader will discern, at this point, that the idea that the unconscious is compensatory contains the germ of one of the concepts for which Jung has been most criticized. The physical sciences have concentrated on causality, and have, so far as is possible, banished teleology from their scheme of things. Thus, in describing the motions of the planets, it has been thought unnecessary and unscientific to ask to what end they perform their elliptic convolutions. In line with this, Freud concentrated on tracing symptoms back to their origins, and seldom asked whether they might be serving a positive function, or pointing the way to a new and possibly better adaptation. Adler, on the other hand, built his psychology around the idea of 'goals'; and interpreted many symptoms in terms of goals (e.g. superiority) towards which the patient was striving. If the idea of compensation is accepted, it is but a short step to the idea that neurotic symptoms may be forward, as well as backward looking. (In Chapter 2, I drew attention to the fact that Jung considered schizophrenic delusional symptoms in a similar light: as abortive attempts at a new and better adaptation). In the example given above, the realization that her mother could be a menace as well as a protection might be taken as pointing the way to a better adaptation in which the girl would become more independent of her mother.

Moreover, if dreams and symptoms can be forward-looking in the way postulated, it is another short step to regarding them as anticipatory. By this, I do not mean that Jung habitually regarded dreams as foretelling the future in any simplistic way (although on occasion he would not have ruled out such a possibility). But he did consider that much psychopathological material contained the seeds of future possibilities, rather than being merely wish-fulfilments or derivatives of the patient's infantile past; and I do not think there is anything in the least unscientific in this supposition.

The idea that the psyche is self-regulating also contains the notion that there is something within the person which 'knows better' than the conscious self; and we have already come across this idea when considering Jung's account of his own self-analysis, and, more especially, in considering what he meant by the archetype of the wise old man. However, there is no need to personify the something which knows better, or to use religious or mystical terminology. Since the time of the physiologist Claude Bernard, scientists have been perfectly used to accepting the idea that the body is a self-regulating entity. Human physiology is governed by an internal system of checks and balances which ensure that any tendency to go too far in one direction is compensated by an opposing swing in the other. Thus, if the blood becomes too alkaline mechanisms are set in operation by which the kidney excretes more alkali and retains acid, thus ensuring that the chemical composition of the blood does not stray too far from its proper mean. The endocrine system is a highly complicated arrangement of self-regulating mechanisms. For example, the pituitary secretes a hormone which stimulates the thyroid gland to produce its own hormone, thyroxine. The more thyroxine there is in the blood, the less will the pituitary produce its thyroid-stimulating hormone. In the terminology of cybernetics, this is a negative feedback, aimed at ensuring that the right amount of thyroxine is always in circulation. Sometimes the mechanisms go wrong, as in thyrotoxicosis or other diseases; but on the whole, the physiology of man is wonderfully well arranged so that his 'internal environment' keeps constant in spite of fluctuations in, and varying exchange with, the world outside. In physiology, the tendency to seek equilibrium is known as 'homeostasis'.

There is nothing intrinsically improbable in supposing that the mind functions in a similar fashion. Jung concluded that the conscious and unconscious balanced each other in reciprocal relation; and that neurosis often served a positive function in that it derived from an attempt on the part of the unconscious to compensate for a one-sided, and hence unhealthy, conscious attitude.

We have already drawn attention to extraversion versus introversion as one example of this self-regulating conception. It is the extreme extravert, apparently only interested in hard facts, who gets suddenly caught by an irrational idea, like some scientists who become ardent spiritualists or dedicated Communists. It is the one-sided intellectual who has never valued emotion who becomes infatuated with a feather-headed actress. Within the ascetic is a sensualist trying to get out; and the persona of the Don Juan may conceal a secret moralist.

The capacity for one-sided development is related to man's complexity, and aptitude for dissociation. The enormous hypertrophy of the human cerebral cortex has enabled man to conquer the world by means of conceptual thought; but it has also made possible a degree of alienation from instinct from which less 'intellectual' creatures are happily debarred. Jung took little apparent interest in the study of animal behaviour, or in physiology. Had he done so, I think he would have found support for both his ideas on self-regulation, and also on dissociation. The neurophysiologist Paul MacClean has shown how the 'old' and the 'new' brains within man can become disconnected, and relates man's peculiar psychology to this lack of inner co-ordination.

Jung maintained that his typology of extravert and introvert was a classification of the normal. Either type could, of course, become neurotic or psychotic; the extravert because he tended to lose touch with his inner world and the introvert because he might lose touch with external reality. There is a good deal to be said for this point of view, but it leaves out of account one important consideration.

As Jung observed, when extraverts become ill, they develop hysterical symptoms; and these symptoms are usually understandable in Freudian terms as derived from a disturbance – more especially, a sexual disturbance – in the patient's relationships with real people in the external world. Jung has little to say specifically upon the manic-depressive psychosis, but I think he would have agreed with most observers in concluding that this, more serious condition, was also a disorder of extraverts.

In Fairbairn's view, the personality of extraverts (whom he would have called 'depressive') is organized in terms of defences against depression. Depression, of immobilizing intensity, is the psychotic condition to which extraverts are liable, and which they most earnestly seek to avoid. Depression, in this, and also in Freud's view, is related to turning inwards against the self aggressive impulses which were originally directed against a loved person in the immediate environment. The extraverted, depressive person, has therefore reached a stage of emotional development in which objects are intensely important to him (indeed, he is over-dependent upon them) but in which he has difficulty in disposing of his aggressive impulses towards others. These aggressive impulses are obviously closely related to Adler's will-to-power, and are also concerned with preserving the subject's independence. As I wrote above, the extravert's difficulty with objects can also be described as an over-involvement in which he loses his own identity.

When introverts become ill, they develop obsessional symptoms; and these symptoms are understandable in terms of power. It is characteristic of obsessionals to want to have everything, both within themselves and in the external world, organized and under their complete control. The power of the subject is paramount, and dependence upon the object reduced as far as possible.

In Fairbairn's scheme of things, the personality of introverts (whom he would have called 'schizoid') is organized in terms of defences against a schizoid state of emotional isolation, characterized by a sense of apathy and loss of meaning rather than depression. The extreme of this state is schizophrenia. According to Fairbairn, the introverted person's difficulty in relating to objects is not merely one of disposing of his aggressive impulses, but of dealing with his loving impulses as well. For this type, even love is dangerous, since loving places him to some extent in the power of another person who might overwhelm or injure him.

Both extraversion and introversion, in the view of Fairbairn and other psychoanalysts, including Melanie Klein and Winnicott, take origin from 'fixations' consequent upon the infant's actual experience in the early months of life. Fairbairn, comparing his own classification with Jung's, alleges that Jung did not consider that psychopathological factors entered into the formation of his types, thus implying that he must have considered them as genetically determined. In fact, Jung seems to have left the question open. Considering the difficulty of proving the validity of Fairbairn or Klein's view of what goes on in the earliest months of the infant's existence, Jung was probably wise not to commit himself. In this connection it is relevant to observe that Jung showed remarkably little interest in the psychopathology of childhood. He was inclined to the view that children were likely to grow up well enough if they were not interfered with, and that if a child did show disturbance it was the psychotherapist's job to treat the parents rather than the child itself. There is very little indeed to be found specifically upon the psychology of children throughout the Collected Works of Jung; although the curious may turn to Vol. 17 where they will find most of the relevant material.

When considering the categories of 'archetype' and 'internal object' we concluded that any dispute as to the origin of the images to which these categories may give rise was of merely theoretical interest. In examining the differences between the schools about the origin of types, however, we come upon a difference which is more important. Jung attempted to put extraversion and introversion upon an equal footing, on the basis that a man needed to relate both to his inner world, and thus to 'introvert' his libido; and also to make connection with the outer world, and thus 'extravert' his libido. Jung's typology does not include the idea that the personality structure underlying introversion is more 'pathological' than that underlying extraversion.

Psychoanalysis, on the other hand, would certainly consider that the extremes of extraversion were less pathological than the extremes of introversion. The ill extravert may become depressed or manic; but these states, however abnormal, do not represent so profound a disturbance as does schizophrenia. This point of view is borne out by the fact that nearly all manic-depressive patients recover, at any rate from any given attack of their disorder, whereas schizophrenics show a strong tendency to become chronic inmates of mental hospitals. In the psychoanalytic view, the extravert who becomes ill regresses to an infantile emotional stage which Melanie Klein calls the 'depressive position'; whereas the introvert who becomes ill regresses to a still earlier point of emotional fixation, the 'paranoid-schizoid' position. This is close to the hypothetical condition of earliest infancy, in which the infant has only the sketchiest awareness of objects in the external world at all, and thus has relationships only with his 'internal objects'.

Both views have something to be said for them. Jung compared extraversion and introversion with the systole and diastole of the normal heart-beat. He would have pointed to the fact that, every night, each of us becomes so introverted during sleep that we enter, in dreams, a subjective world principally governed by what is inside rather than what is outside. He would, I think, have been not at all surprised by modern electroencephalographic research into sleep, which has shown that dreams are necessary if psychological stability is to be preserved. On the other hand, it is true that the extremes of introversion are more pathological than the extremes of extraversion. Schizophrenics are undoubtedly iller than manic-depressives in that they have more completely abandoned their links with external reality; and the hypothesis that this represents a more profound regression is a likely one. Jung's lack of any convincing historical scheme of infantile development, however hypothetical, is actually a weakness when his ideas are compared with psychoanalytic theory.

A great deal of the difference between the two points of view hinges upon different conceptions of the inner world of the psyche. Psychoanalysts consider that the inner world and its images are infantile phenomena; admittedly powerful determinants of a man's idea of the external world, and therefore of his behaviour, but actually a hindrance in adaptation to reality. The mythological level of the psyche is, in this view, a misconstruction which ought to be outgrown or overgrown if a person is to be properly orientated towards people in an adult way, and towards the external world as it actually is. The weakness of this point of view is that it fails to explain why we need to regress in sleep or passive reverie.

Jung, on the other hand, puts the inner world of myth and archetype upon an equal footing with the external world. He sees the ego poised, as it were, between inner and outer, between subjective and objective, with an equal need to relate to each world. The idea that the inner world is in any sense infantile or pathological appears to be alien to him.

Neither Jung nor the psychoanalysts consider the possibility that man's inner world of myth and fantastic image may be both a residue of infancy and also adaptive in the biological sense; a hypothesis advanced by the present author, and briefly referred to in the last chapter.

Man's primary task, like that of other animals, must surely be to make the best possible adaptation to the external world in which he finds himself. But man's peculiar, and highly successful, adaptation is partially indirect; by means of abstraction, symbol, and conceptual thought. To motivate this adaptation he needs an inner world of phantasy which cannot easily or directly be satisfied in instinctual fashion. Religion, culture, art, science, and all the other specifically human adaptations to the external world can be thought of as originating from this source. Obviously, this is not the place to pursue this particular notion. But it is appropriate to draw attention to the fact that both the psychoanalytic and the Jungian concepts of man's inner world contain some measure of truth, and that further thought is needed upon how to reconcile these opposites.

Jung's point of view is, of course, introverted, as he himself acknowledged. But although introverted, it is poles apart from that of Alfred Adler. One must accept Jung's own statement that it was consideration of the Adlerian, as opposed to the Freudian, point of view which prompted Jung's formulation of his type theory; but Adler is actually a rather poor example of what is generally thought of as an introvert. Adler certainly emphasized the superiority of the subject at the expense of the object; but he hardly acknowledged the existence of an inner world or 'unconscious' – and believed that man's salvation was to be found in social co-operation. Adler's basic notion of the 'will-to-power' gradually changed its nomenclature through 'striving for superiority' to 'striving towards perfection': and this latter ideal was only to be achieved in an ideal society of co-operating human beings all motivated by a common search for this perfection. Perhaps Adler may be considered as a good example of Jung's thesis that a man's type can change. Certainly Adler's theoretical views seem to have become more and more extraverted as he got older.

Having delineated extraversion and introversion, Jung proceeded to subdivide his types into four further categories, based upon the supposed predominance of sensation, thinking, feeling, or intuition. Each category could apply to either extraverts or introverts, so that there came to be eight types in all.

Jung argued as follows. Sensation is the function by which men realize that a thing exists. 'Sensation tells me that something *is*: it does not tell me *what* it is and it does not tell me other things about that something; it only tells me that something is.'

Thinking is the function by which one tells what a thing is. 'It gives a name to the thing. It adds a concept, because thinking is perception and judgement.'

Feeling, in Jung's view, is concerned with questions of value. 'Feeling tells you for instance whether a thing is acceptable or agreeable or not. It tells you what a thing is *worth* to you.'

Intuition is concerned with time. The intuitive person is able to 'see round corners', to have hunches about things, and is more interested in the possibilities of things than in their present existence.[5]

Jung considered that, just as either extraversion or introversion tended to be the predominant attitude of any given individual, so either thinking, feeling, sensation, or intuition tended to be the predominant function. He further postulated that thinking was opposed to feeling, and sensation to intuition. This meant that the person who was chiefly adapted to the world through thinking would be likely to function poorly in matters of feeling. The man who was always sensing future possibilities in things through intuition would be likely to be deficient in his appreciation of their concrete reality by means of sensation. This makes a neat scheme of conflicting oppo-

sites which balance one another. The theoretically perfectly adapted individual would be the person in whom
none of the functions predominated at the expense of its
opposite, but to whom all were equally available as conditions demanded.

I think it is fair to say that this further classification of
types is one of Jung's least satisfactory contributions, in
spite of the fact that the description of the eight different
types which occurs at the end of 'Psychological Types'
makes good reading. It has always been recognized that
there is some opposition between reason and emotion.
As I observed above, it is the 'intellectual' who tends to
get caught out by his irrational feelings; and dons are
notorious amongst analysts as being difficult patients,
since they are apt to exhibit obsessional, intellectual defences against experiencing emotion. But there is considerable overlap between what Jung calls 'feeling' and
his notions of 'sensation' and 'intuition'. Intuition may
often be explained in terms of the person exhibiting it
being sensitive to, and picking up subliminal cues in the
environment of which he is not consciously aware. To
do so requires a sensory apparatus of a high order which
registers reality accurately. This registration, however,
should come under the heading of 'sensation', not be
opposed to it. In Jung's terminology, determining value
is a function of feeling. But how, for instance, in making
an aesthetic judgement, are we to separate feeling and
sensation? If I am to accept a person's evaluation of,
say, a piece of music, I expect him first of all to have a
good ear, a feature which surely belongs to the area of
sensation. I also, incidentally, expect him to be able to
think. Even in the realm of scientific thinking Jung's
separation of these functions is not always appropriate.
As G. H. Hardy has pointed out in 'A Mathematician's
Apology', beauty and seriousness are two criteria by
which mathematical theorems are, and should be,

judged. In Jung's terminology, such judgements are matters of feeling. Yet one can hardly suppose that a mathematical theorem can be created without thought, so that Jung's idea that thinking and feeling are necessarily incompatible is not borne out. In one lecture, Jung illustrated what he meant with a diagram; E standing for ego, T for thinking, F for feeling, S for sensation, and I for intuition.[6]

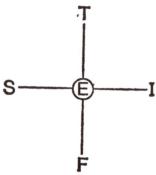

This is an interesting diagram if considered in terms of a topic with which we shall deal later; the mandala as representing a new synthesis or irrational union of opposites. Mandalas are generally circular forms or else have a quaternary structure. I think Jung's diagram of the four functions is a rudimentary and premature realization of the theme which preoccupied him all his life, and to which I drew attention in the first chapter; the reconciliation of opposing forces within the personality. Creative people who are good at making patterns sometimes crystallize their patterns prematurely, because it is so intrinsically satisfying to make a new one. My own view is that the opposition of the four functions is too neat a pattern, which is actually of little help in grasping how different personalities perceive the world; but this assessment may be too harsh.

Jung classified himself as an introverted thinker,

whose next best function to thinking was intuition. He says of himself: 'I had a definite difficulty with feeling, and my relation to reality was not particularly brilliant.'[7] Perhaps this is why, in his diagram reproduced above, thinking is placed at the top, and intuition pictured on the right; whereas feeling is relegated to the bottom, and sensation placed on the left (in Jungian terminology, the side of the unconscious). It is arguable that Jung was more of a feeling, and less of a thinking, type than he recognized. He generally made an excellent rapport with those he met; surely, in his terms, a matter of feeling. But almost everyone who has attempted a critical assessment of Jung has come to the conclusion that his thinking was confused, that he contradicts himself, uses words in differing senses, and often makes use of 'blanket' concepts which include so much under a single heading that they actually explain less than at first appears. Whilst the dichotomy of extraversion versus introversion has proved valuable and continues to stimulate research, the quaternity of the four functions has been discarded by all except the most dedicated Jungians, and is, I suspect, little used even by them.

5 The Process of Individuation

As we have seen, Jung was, throughout his life, pre-occupied with the problem of reconciling opposites within himself. In youth, he had felt himself to be an awkward lad, and at the same time, possessed of authority and wisdom. As a student, he had wondered how he could reconcile his 'subjective' need for his own Weltan-schauung with the 'objective' requirements of science. As a young adult, he saw the same problem in his schizophrenic patients, who needed their delusional myths, but, at the same time, should also have been able to relate to the world outside. Then came his encounter with Freud and Adler, the extravert and the introvert. Both were right, yet their points of view conflicted. It seemed important to be able to take a stand in which one was not wholly identified with either subjective or objective; with extraversion or introversion; or even with good or evil. Man was both flesh and spirit; reason and emotion; saint and sinner; and, in Jung's view, the whole energy of mental functioning sprang from tension between these opposites. In the last chapter, we saw that many of the physiological systems of the body are set in motion as compensatory devices, just as fatigue compels sleep, or a lowered blood sugar causes food-seeking. Physiological activity springs from imbalance yet centres around a balanced mean, constantly sought, departed from as soon as achieved, hardly definable, yet omnipresent in the background.

Towards the end of the first World War, Jung began to emerge from his period of mental upheaval. Like other creative people emerging from a mid-life crisis, he achieved a sense of acceptance and finality. His phantasies, which by then he had begun to draw and paint, altered in character. Instead of images of persons, Jung became preoccupied with abstract, circular patterns, often subdivided into four or some multiple of that number. These patterns, which, as he later discovered, were similar to those used for meditation and known as mandalas in the East, seemed to symbolize his achievement of a new balance within his own psyche; a balance in which there was some reconciliation between the opposing forces which had been tearing him apart. The journey towards this new integration came to be known as the process of individuation; and the mandala patterns in which it was expressed symbolized a new centre within the psyche which was neither conscious nor unconscious but partook of both. This centre Jung named the Self.

The process of individuation is, as Jung said himself, the central concept of his psychology. It is, I think, his major contribution and, as such, deserves detailed exposition and comment. This is not an easy task, since Jung's writings on the subject are obscure, and he fails to relate his ideas to other schools of analytic thought. Some of what I have to say might well have not appealed to Jung himself and will, no doubt, be disputed by those of his immediate circle who still survive at the time of writing. Controversy, however, may often prove an aid to understanding; or, as Jung would have put it, quoting Heraclitus, 'War is the father of all.'

The first thing to realize about individuation is that it is essentially a process which takes place in the second half of life. Moreover, it is an esoteric process which engages only the few. 'It would also be a great mistake to suppose that this is the path every neurotic must travel, or that it is the solution at every stage of the neurotic problem. It is appropriate only in those cases where consciousness has reached an abnormal degree of development and has diverged too far from the unconscious. This is the *sine qua non* of the process. Nothing would be more wrong than to open this way to neurotics who are ill on account of an excessive predominance of the unconscious. For the same reason, this way of development has scarcely any meaning before the middle of life (normally between the ages of thirty-five and forty), and if entered upon too soon can be decidedly injurious.'[1]

This is a time of life which used to be, although it no longer is, neglected by Freudians, who were wary of taking into analysis persons of middle age and over. Psychoanalysis has always been chiefly concerned with neurotics who, in Jung's phrase, suffer from 'an excessive predominance of the unconscious', or, to say the same thing in different words, suffer from a weak ego. It is often forgotten that Freud defined neuroses as 'disorders of the ego'; and Fenichel states the same thing even more clearly when he wrote: 'All neurotic phenomena are based on insufficiencies of the normal control apparatus.'[2] Jung's patients did not lack control, and possessed strong egos. In fact, they were a special group, unlike the general run of neurotics encountered in the ordinary psychotherapeutic practice. In one passage Jung writes: 'Most of my patients are socially well-adapted individuals, often of outstanding ability, to whom normalization means nothing.'[3] In another he states: 'The clinical material at my disposal is of a peculiar composition: new cases are decidedly in the minority. Most of them already have some form of psychotherapeutic treatment behind them, with partial or negative results. About a third of my cases are not suffering from any clinically definable neurosis, but from the senselessness and aimlessness of their lives. I should not object if this were called the general neurosis of our age. Fully two-thirds of my patients are in the second half of life.'[4]

In what follows, it is important to bear in mind the special characteristics of this group. Although some Jungians would argue that the individuation process is a natural course of development which takes place in everyone, for the most part unconsciously, it was Jung's experience first with himself, and second with this sophisticated and unusual group of patients which led to his defining the process. The modern school of existential analysts would, I believe, refer to these patients as 'alienated'; a concept closely similar to Jung's idea of consciousness diverging too far from the unconscious.

In Jung's view, the individual's task during the first half of life was to establish himself in the world, sever the childhood ties which bound him to his parents, gain himself a mate, and start a new family. Jung often refers to these tasks as 'fulfilling one's obligations'; and one gains the impression that, for him, the struggles of individuals to achieve these ends were not of much intrinsic interest. Most psychotherapeutic practices consist principally of individuals who have been unsuccessful in emancipating themselves from childhood and establishing happy heterosexual relationships; hence the Freudian goal, already referred to, of 'genitality'; that is, of a mature heterosexual relationship as being the touchstone of both adulthood and freedom from neurosis. Jung constantly reiterated that Freudian psychology, or Adlerian for that matter, were perfectly applicable to the problems of most young persons. These points of view, however, were not so satisfactory when one came face to face with the problems of the second half of life; and it was then that his particular contribution came into its own. This is true if one confines oneself to considering Freudian and Adlerian psychology as promulgated before the first World War. It is not so true subsequently. I have already made reference to Elliott Jaques' paper 'Death and the Mid-Life Crisis'. This, written from the Kleinian standpoint, shows that modern psychoanalysts are well aware of the problems with which Jung was dealing, though they use quite different terminology. The problems of the second half of life are referred to by Jaques in terms of working through the 'depressive position', and coming to terms with death.[5] But, as I have said, Jung's interest in Freud and Adler seems to have ceased with his own separation from the former.

In Jungian terms, the tasks of the first half of life are symbolized by the mythologem of the hero, to which I made brief reference at the end of Chapter 2. But what happens when the hero has emancipated himself from the past, proved his (Adlerian) power, and gained his (Freudian) mate? Sometimes he is killed, or even sacrifices himself. In a dream which he had on December 18th, 1913, Jung describes how he had to take part in the killing of Siegfried, who is, of course, a typical hero figure. Another is Osiris, who having established his kingdom in Egypt, is also killed. After his resurrection he prefers to reign in an Egyptian Elysian Fields rather than return to earth. Christ is sacrificed on the Cross, and is transported to a kingdom 'not of this world'. Perhaps the ego's achievement of power and sexual happiness was not enough, at any rate for human beings to whom such gains were easy. Perhaps the death of the hero could be taken as signifying a turning-point in life at which the ego has to relinquish the seat of power, and acknowledge its dependence upon something or someone greater than itself.

I wrote in chapter 1 that, for Freud, the ego remained firmly in the driver's seat as the most important part of the personality, and that the object of psychoanalysis was to convert id into ego. It is significant that it was the last chapter of 'Symbols of Transformation' about which

Jung hesitated so long; because it is this chapter, called 'The Sacrifice' which has to do with the death of the hero. Jung's wife believed that Freud would accept this chapter, but Jung knew better. For in it is the notion that man may be a creature who has to withdraw some of his emotional investment from the pursuit of the mundane goals of power and sexual happiness in favour of a spiritual goal beyond this world. In retrospect, it is curious that Freud did not accept some such notion, in view of the fact that he wrote to a correspondent at the age of only forty-one saying that sexual excitement was of no further use to him. It is clear that, for Freud, the pursuit of truth as he saw it became the main goal of the second half of his life; and this pursuit could equally be regarded as 'spiritual'. For Freud, however, sublimation remained a substitute for the 'real thing', not an essential part of development.

Jung's own sacrifice of mundane goals was the abandonment of his academic career, which took place in the midst of his mid-life crisis and self-analysis. He said himself that he was glad he did not become a professor at this stage of his life; but that he knew what sacrifice meant.

Jung, I think, believed that the 'heroic' achievements of the first half of life were inevitably accompanied by a certain one-sidedness. This is the period of life when the individual makes use of his 'superior function' to gain his ends; and when his typology is apt to be exaggerated. The busy, successful man of affairs is so intent on his pursuit of wealth and power that he has no time to give to the cultivation of his inner life. The scholar, although apparently more inward-looking, may, in his exclusive preoccupation with intellectual matters, become equally divorced from the springs of feeling and emotion. As Jung says, many of his patients were both intelligent and successful. It is just when success has been achieved, often, in Western civilization, at about the mid-point of life, that a man begins to ask whether there might not be more to life than success, and what the meaning of his existence may be. If a man is to reach serenity and that harmony within himself which, for Jung, became the goal of life, he must rediscover those aspects of himself which have been neglected; and to do this requires the partial sacrifice of the very function or attitude which served him well and brought him success in the early years. Thus both the power-seeker and the intellectual need to correct their one-sided development; and the way in which this is done is first by paying attention to, and second by coming to understand, the spontaneous productions of the unconscious as expressed in dream and phantasy. The analysis of this particular group, there-fore, had to concern itself not only with the Freudian goal of love and the Adlerian goal of power, but with the underlying, and generally unconscious attitude to both these drives. This, inevitably, leads both analyst and patient to a consideration of values. Adlerian man and Freudian man are not so 'scientific' as they appear, since neither is able to avoid making value judgements, al-though these may be implicit rather than overt. For the one, 'superiority' represents the supreme value; for the other, sexuality. In Jung's view, when it came to dealing with serious psychological problems, it was impossible to avoid a discussion of this underlying attitude, or Weltanschauung, as he would have called it. Moreover, it was equally impossible for an individual not to have some kind of Weltanschauung, even if he had never formulated it, and was thus unconscious of it. We are all influenced, whether we like it or not, by the collective assumptions of the age we live in; by the general atti-tudes to such things as sex, power, democracy, beauty, science, and many other things which we tend to take for granted. Yet, in other historical periods, men of equal intelligence have made assumptions differing from our own. For example, in the twentieth century in America and Western Europe, it might be alleged that there was, until recently, a rather general assumption that what most people were aiming at throughout the world was an improvement in their standards of living; and that the rapid progress of science would be likely to bring this about. Now, faced with a world threatened with destruction by pollution, and under the perpetual threat of the hydrogen bomb, we are not so sure. There is a perceptible change in the collective attitude towards science; a realization that more is not necessarily better, and a general shift towards considering what should be the quality of life. As we have seen, the patients in whom Jung became most interested were alienated people who were, in effect, disenchanted with the goals of 'honour, power, wealth, fame, and the love of women', as Freud put it.[6] What goal, and what values had analysis to offer such people?

For Jung, the supreme value, the goal towards which the individual's psychological development was tending, was that of integration or 'wholeness'. The person who has achieved this goal possesses, in Jung's words, 'an attitude that is beyond the reach of emotional entanglements and violent shocks – a consciousness detached from the world.'[7] In Jung's view, and here I think that Kleinians like Elliott Jaques would agree with him, such an attitude, achieved only in the second half of life, is a preparation for death. A certain degree of detachment from the world is, of course, valuable when one is preparing to leave it for ever: and this has been amply recognized by both Christianity and Buddhism. What is interesting is that Jung, and later analysts studying the mid-life crisis, have concluded that this preoccupation with death begins so early, and that it is a natural part of the individual's psychological development. I see no reason to suppose that they are wrong.

The conscious attitude which accompanies the achievement of this new integration is essentially one of acceptance; more especially, of ceasing to do violence to one's own nature by repressing any side of it, or by over-developing any particular aspect. In his commentary on 'The Secret of the Golden Flower' Jung quotes a letter from a former patient which illustrates what he means.

'Out of evil, much good has come to me. By keeping quiet, repressing nothing, remaining attentive, and by accepting reality – taking things as they are, and not as I wanted them to be – by doing all this, unusual knowledge has come to me, and unusual powers as well, such as I could never have imagined before. I always thought that when we accepted things they overpowered us in some way or other. This turns out not to be true at all, and it is only by accepting them that one can assume an attitude towards them. So now I intend to play the game of life, being receptive to whatever comes to me, good and bad, sun and shadow for ever alternating, and, in this way, also accepting my own nature with its positive and negative sides. Thus everything becomes more alive to me. What a fool I was! How I tried to force everything to go according to the way I thought it ought to!'[8]

Jung calls such an attitude 'religious', although the person who achieves it may not subscribe to any of the recognized creeds. By sacrificing the ego's mundane goals, and accepting what comes, the individual is acknowledging dependence on something beyond the ego, which lives in and through him. It will be recalled that, in the Jungian scheme of things, there is a self-regulating principle within the mind, just as there is within the body. This self-regulating principle manifests itself in varying ways; in dreams, for example, or even in neurotic symptoms which force the individual to take notice of what is going on inside him. The attitude of paying careful attention to whatever comes, and of acceptance would, I think, be described by religious people as 'waiting upon God'.

Thus the analysis of people in the second half of life became, for Jung, a spiritual quest or journey. Indeed, he said quite openly that analysis was a religious experience. During the course of his own self-analysis, Jung had finally succeeded in finding what he had been looking for since childhood, his own 'myth'; a myth which gave his life purpose and value, which incorporated Christian values and yet was not conventional Christianity, and which brought about a reconciliation between the conflicting sides of his own nature.

It will be recalled that, as a child, Jung had started to rebel against the old-fashioned, orthodox Christianity in which he had been reared. Indeed, in his autobiographical reminiscences, he describes a vision of God obscenely destroying his own cathedral, and a dream dating from very early childhood, of an underground phallic deity. In adolescence, he had attempted, without avail, to make his father respond to his religious doubts and queries. During his mid-life crisis, as often happens, he was forced into a regression in which his childhood problems once more came to the surface. The eventual answer which came to him was the process of individuation. This could be described as a kind of Pilgrim's Progress without a creed, aiming not at heaven, but at integration and wholeness. It was something to live by, and yet it was neither a schizophrenic delusion nor a primitive myth, nor yet an orthodox faith. The end result of the process was becoming an integrated individual, a fully-developed personality in one's own right.

This, to many people, will seem an ignoble and self-centred aim. One literary critic reviewing 'Memories, Dreams, Reflections' refers to Jung's 'insane self-absorption'; and indeed, this ill-considered autobiography about which Jung himself was highly dubious, invites criticism of this kind. There does, at first sight, seem something distasteful about anyone making the development of his own personality into a kind of religion. It is, of course, a criticism which could be, and often is, aimed at varieties of analysis other than Jungian. 'Spending all that time and money on yourself' is an accusation levelled at Freudian analysands as well. Moreover, Jung himself was exceedingly bad at putting his ideas across. I gave above a rather sketchy outline of the kind of *conscious* attitude to be expected in a person who had reached a new stage of integration as a result of analysis. I said nothing about the unconscious process, exhibited in dream and phantasy, by which this new integration is brought about. But it was this 'unconscious' process which fascinated Jung, and it is writings on this process which constitute the bulk of his later work. He writes next to nothing about the effect of analysis upon the patient's life in the world or upon his personal relationships. Obviously, if a person becomes happier, more balanced, more integrated, one expects that his personal relationships will improve. One might also hope that he would become better at his job, or take up a new career. But Jung says nothing about all this. It is difficult to avoid the impression that many of Jung's patients were either analysts in training, or else successful people with money to spare who were able to devote an unconscionable amount of time to pursuing their own inner development because they were free both of family responsibilities and financial anxieties. Just as Jung says practically nothing about his relationships with his wife or other women in his autobiography, so, in discussing his patients, he tells us about their dreams and phantasies, but next to nothing about the persons to whom these dreams and phantasies occurred. This is one reason why the Collected Works of Jung discourage the average reader. Unless he is exceptionally persistent, he is unlikely to find anything which seems remotely connected with day-to-day problems, neurotic symptoms, sexual difficulties, and all the other matters which may make a person turn to books on psychology and psychotherapy. Unless one is already fairly familiar with Jung's point of view, it is frustrating to open one of his books and be confronted with a discussion of 'The Visions of Zosimos' or a disquisition upon the meaning of the Trinity.

It is important to realize that Jung, like other people who have come upon a good idea, wanted to find support and justification for it. It is only schizophrenics who *know* they are right; and who do not seek or expect to find any outside support for their delusional system. Indeed, this is one criterion for distinguishing a delusional system from a myth or religious belief. Moreover, Jung had a lively historical sense. As we have seen, he thought that the nature of man did not change much in the course of centuries. Other people, therefore, perhaps at other periods of history, must have felt and thought as he did himself. Was there evidence of other people pursuing an inner path of development, analogous to the individuation process, and reaching the same goal of a new integration?

In 1928 the sinologist, Richard Wilhelm, sent Jung a Taoist text, 'The Secret of the Golden Flower' which seemed to him to describe a process of psychological development closely similar to that which he had passed through himself, and which he now observed in his patients. Within a year or two, he found additional confirmation for his views in the study of medieval alchemy. Until Jung made alchemy more or less respectable, it was usually dismissed as pre-scientific superstition; an incomprehensible collection of dubious recipes which were aimed at transmitting base metals into gold. There is no doubt that the alchemists were mostly serious people who did in fact conduct chemical experiments. Since, however, there was no chemical science which could explain what was happening in the changes in matter which they encountered, they sought analogies between their own human experience and what they noticed in the laboratory. Thus, the combining of two dissimilar substances was described as a 'marriage' and the production of a third thereby as a 'birth'. The alchemists were much concerned with the perfecting of matter, which, to them, was analogous to the perfecting of man in fulfilling the laws of God. With the rise of natural science in the seventeenth century, such ideas became untenable, and alchemy divided into two branches, the one becoming the science of chemistry, and the other a religious philosophy. Before this Cartesian division, however, the subjective and the objective were inextricably mingled, so that what the alchemists described was partly what went on in the laboratory, and partly what went on in themselves. If one likes so to describe it, there was both an extraverted and an introverted side to alchemy. Jung, true to his own nature, concentrated wholly upon the introverted aspect. He saw alchemy as a process of inner, psychological development in the alchemist himself, and the chemical changes and new combinations as changes within the personality. For a more extraverted view, the reader is referred to F. Sherwood Taylor's book, 'The Alchemists', in which more attention is given to alchemy as a precursor of chemistry,[9] and in which Jung is criticized for concentrating only upon one aspect.

There is a famous and frequently used personality test, invented by the psychologist Rorschach, which consists of presenting the subject with a series of cards upon which are a series of standardized ink-blots. Since an ink-blot is not in itself significant, anything which the subject sees in it must be a reflection of his own psychology;

a projection, in fact, of something from within. Jung's view of alchemy is easily grasped if it is recognized that he regarded it as a gigantic Rorschach test. Alchemy was not chemistry, and there was therefore 'nothing in it'; nothing that is, except the projection of the psychological process of the experimenter. The alchemists, like Jung and his patients, were engaged upon a spiritual progress, a search for integration and individuation. This is not the place to expand upon the analogies which Jung found between his own conceptions and the various stages of the alchemical process. The curious are referred to the twelfth volume of the Collected Works, 'Psychology and Alchemy', and, more especially to the introduction to this volume, which is more comprehensible and better expressed than much of Jung's other writing. The concept which we must now consider is Jung's idea of the Self.

6 The Concept of the Self

In an interesting passage, again taken from his commentary on 'The Secret of the Golden Flower', Jung describes how some of his patients, faced with what appeared to be an insoluble conflict, solved it by 'outgrowing' it, by developing 'a new level of consciousness'. He writes: 'Some higher or wider interest appeared on the patient's horizon, and through this broadening of his outlook the insoluble problem lost its urgency. It was not solved logically in its own terms, but faded out when confronted with a new and stronger life urge.'[1]

The attainment of this new level of psychological development includes a certain degree of the detachment discussed in the last chapter; in this case detachment from one's own emotions. 'One certainly does feel the affect and is shaken and tormented by it, yet at the same time one is aware of a higher consciousness looking on which prevents one from becoming identical with the affect, a consciousness which regards the affect as an object, and can say, "*I know* that I suffer".'[2]

Characteristically, Jung gives no concrete example of what he means by an insoluble problem, no case-history of an actual individual which might serve as an illustration of what he means. Let us, therefore, guess what he means by taking a common example of an 'insoluble' conflict from psychotherapeutic practice. A middle-aged man with high ethical standards who is reasonably happily married falls passionately in love with a younger woman. If he runs off with her he does violence to his own standards of loyalty, morality, and justice; if he stays with his family he does violence to the most compelling emotion he has ever experienced. It is no use denying either the one or the other; for, even if he succeeds in expelling the younger woman from his life, he will suffer depression and resentment and thus 'take it out' on his family. Such 'insoluble conflicts' are all too common; but are usually solved in the obvious way either by the man staying at home and feeling permanently resentful; or else by his going off and feeling for ever guilty. What Jung is saying is that, provided the man can detach himself from both sets of emotions, there is a third possibility. His conflict can be solved by 'developing a new level of consciousness'; that is, upon a symbolic level.

In Jungian terms, the man's first task would be to differentiate the young woman from the image which he is projecting upon her; that is, to recognize the subjective nature of his infatuation. If he sees the woman as she actually is, then he will also recognize the 'anima'; the image which originates from within his own psyche. Once this is done, the path is open for an *internal* process of development, beginning with those dialogues with the anima and other archetypal figures of which Jung was so fond, and which seem peculiar to those who are not Jungians. In other words, this is a technique which precludes 'acting out' emotions in the external world, and transfers the conflict to the inner world of the psyche. Instead of the woman in the external world appearing to be 'the answer'; to give meaning and significance to life, emotional significance is transferred to his inner world of feeling. The internal process of development which is thus set in motion is, of course, individuation. As we have already seen, not everyone is suited to pursue this inner path of development. In youth, the passions may be too strong for the conflict to be contained; and so a one-sided, 'acted out' solution in one or other direction may be the only answer. But the kind of patient with whom Jung was concerned was not only middle-aged, but comparatively robust psychologically: and therefore possessed the capacity for suffering the conflict and containing the dissonant emotions. It is only when a person is tough enough to tolerate the opposites within that a symbolic solution can make its appearance.

It would, of course, be argued that, ultimately, symbolic solutions are the only appropriate answer to severe emotional problems. Most difficulties in interpersonal relationships – at least between ordinary decent people – are actually referable to the 'inner worlds' of the persons concerned and not to their actual personalities in the world of reality. It is the images from this inner world which are projected upon other people which cause the trouble: and it is coming to terms with these images, or finding some way of dealing with them which is the principal task of any kind of analysis. Therefore, most long-term analyses, whether Jungian or not, are more concerned with symbolic solutions within the psyche itself than with the patient's actions in the external world.

Jung's idea was that, in our theoretical case, a sufficient degree of detachment from feelings (and I mean both the individual's 'moral' feelings and his infatuation) is only possible if the man subordinates his subjectivity to a higher, more objective goal. People who have a living faith in one or other of the orthodox creeds can often do this. The religious person, faced with such a conflict, has a higher authority to whom he can turn, a set of rules or moral principles to which he can subordinate himself, and a promise of eventual redemption and healing, if not in this world, then at least in the next. But what of the person who cannot subscribe to an orthodox creed; who does not believe in a God who will make all well in the end?

In Chapter 3, attempting to explain what Jung meant by archetypes, I quoted his remarks upon 'subjective aptitudes'. Thus the whole nature of man presupposes woman, both physically and spiritually. His system is tuned in to woman from the start, just as it is prepared for a quite definite world where there is water, light, air, salt, carbohydrates, etc. The form of the world into which he is born is already inborn in him as virtual images, as psychic aptitudes. These *a priori* categories have by nature a collective character; they are images of parents, wife, and children in general, and are not individual predestinations.'[8]

In Freud's view, religion should and could be replaced by science. In Jung's belief, this was quite impossible. Man had always needed, and would continue to require, some kind of religion or myth by which to live. If this was so, it followed that, inborn in man, there must be a 'virtual image', a 'psychic aptitude' for God himself. As with other archetypes, this was indefinable in itself, the flexible mould which cannot be seen until filled. God has, throughout history, taken on many shapes and many guises. This archetype Jung named the Self. As he writes in the introduction to 'Psychology and Alchemy', 'the soul must contain in itself the faculty of relation to God, i.e. a correspondence, otherwise a connection could never come about. This correspondence is, in psychological terms, the archetype of the God-image.'[4]

Jung was fond of quoting that ancient father of the Church, Tertullian, who was a pagan until he was about thirty-five, and who then became converted to Christianity; another example of a mid-life crisis. Amongst other dicta, Tertullian alleged that *anima naturaliter christiana*; the soul is naturally Christian; and, although Jung would not have confined the soul's predilection to Christianity, he would have supported the thesis that it was naturally religious. Above the front door of his house in Küsnacht, Jung had carved a saying originally promulgated by the Delphic oracle which, in Latin, rather than the original Greek, states: 'Vocatus atque non vocatus, deus aderit'; that is, 'Invoked or not invoked the god will be present.'

Jung believed that only by recognizing some higher authority than the ego, could a man detach himself sufficiently from sexuality, the will-to-power, and the other compulsions of the world (see the death of the hero in Chapter 5). If a man had no god as a spiritual, inner experience, he would make a god out of something else, be that sex, or power, or even reason. 'To serve a mania is detestable and undignified, but to serve a god is full of meaning and promise because it is an act of submission to a higher, invisible, and spiritual being.'[5] The god which Jung discovered in the unconscious turned out to be something rather different from the God of orthodox Christianity, and Jung had to pursue somewhat obscure researches into Gnosticism, alchemy, and other repositories of *arcana* to support his finding that his own and his patients' experience of 'wholeness', of the union of opposites, of reaching a point above conflict, was also an experience of God.

This of course explains why so much of Jung's later writings are concerned with the problem of evil. Since man is both good and evil, saint and sinner, resolution of his conflicts must include coming to terms with his 'evil' side. But if God represents a union of opposites, then God must also have His evil or dark side. According to Jung, this actually corresponds with what was taught by some early religious authorities. Clement of Rome, for example, alleged that 'God rules the world with a right and left hand, the right being Christ, the left Satan.'[6] As is the case with so much Jungian psychology, the exploration of what at first appear to be relatively simple ideas leads into philosophical and religious problems which are beyond the reach of any but professional philosophers and theologians. Both ignorance and lack of space preclude me from following Jung into the complicated recesses of his arguments with theologians upon the *privatio boni*; his elaborate discussion of Satan as a fallen angel, and his portrayal of the injustice and arbitrary nature of God's dark side in 'Answer to Job'. The inquisitive reader is referred not only to this piece of 'pure poison', as Jung called it; which is to be found in Vol. 11 of the Collected Works, 'Psychology and Religion', but also to 'God and the Unconscious' by Father Victor White, and 'Religion and the Psychology of Jung' by Father Raymond Hostie."[8]

Religious problems of doctrine are so remote from the conceptual framework of the average Western agnostic that many readers will abandon Jung at this point. Nevertheless, Jung was, in my view, in describing the process of individuation and the experience of the Self, drawing attention to something important which does occur in human psychological development; and is not an unrealistic or delusional phantasy. Because for Jung, religious belief, however unorthodox, represented a supreme value, he was unable to conceive of this process in other than religious terms. 'The highest dominant', he writes, 'always has a religious or a philosophical character.'[9] Although this was true for Jung, I do not think it is necessarily true for everyone. Although Jung would probably not have agreed, it is possible to see something closely equivalent to the individuation process in quite another field; and since, in seeking to understand Jung, I have found the analogy illuminating, I assume that some other people may do so also.

During the time of his self-analysis, Jung records that he was from time to time in contact with an 'aesthetic lady' who maintained that his phantasies, and the drawings and paintings in which he enshrined them, were really works of art. Jung was tempted so to regard them; but writes: 'If I had taken these fantasies of the uncon-

scious as art, they would have carried no more conviction than visual perceptions, as if I were watching a
movie. I would have felt no moral obligation towards
them. The anima might then have easily seduced me into
believing that I was a misunderstood artist, and that my
so-called artistic nature gave me the right to neglect
reality.'[10] In a later passage he writes of a letter from
the aesthetic lady 'in which she again stubbornly maintained that the fantasies arising from my unconscious
had artistic value and should be considered art. The
letter got on my nerves. It was far from stupid and
therefore dangerously persuasive. The modern artist,
after all, seeks to create art out of the unconscious. The
utilitarianism and self-importance concealed behind this
thesis touched a doubt in myself, namely, my uncertainty as to whether the fantasies I was producing were
really spontaneous and natural, and not only my own
arbitrary inventions.'[11]

It is obvious, from this passage, that Jung put the production of works of art upon a far lower level than he
did the emergence of religious ideas. And yet it is hard to
see, if one values art, why this should be so. Serious
artists agree that the works which they produce are not
by any means 'arbitrary inventions' of a personal kind.
Moreover, they freely acknowledge that their creations
are shaped by, and take origin from, a source beyond
conscious control. Novelists report that their characters
take on 'lives of their own', and may behave in ways
contrary to the author's original, conscious intention.
Artists also often describe feelings of 'moral obligation'
towards their work, in that they feel compelled to be
true to whatever vision has been vouchsafed to them;
and recognize that, if they try to alter or correct this too
far, disaster follows and the work is a failure.

Graham Wallas, in his description of the creative process, named four stages which have become generally

accepted; preparation, incubation, illumination, verification.[12] These stages are comparable to those described by Jung as belonging to the process of individuation, and are also analogous to some of the stages of 'The Work' delineated by the alchemists. It seems curious that Jung became so irritated with his 'aesthetic lady'. It is true that neither Jung's paintings nor his writings are works of art; but what he describes as taking place in both himself and his patients is closely parallel with what artists describe as the creative process. The fact that Jung and his patients did not produce great art does not, of course, invalidate this thesis. The creative process taking place in bad artists may be much the same as the creative process in good artists, although its results may not be valuable for anyone other than the bad artist himself.

I think Jung's irritation sprang from two different sources. First, although in many ways he was personally humble, he does seem to have believed that his visions, dreams, and phantasies were direct revelations from God. He once said, referring to dreams, 'Every night, one has the chance of the Eucharist.' It will be remembered that, during his period of mental upheaval, Jung was inclined to attribute his own disturbance to a disturbance in the external world. Religious ideas seem, for Jung, to have been in a different category from creative ideas of other varieties, more 'objective' and less 'subjective', no doubt because religion represented to him the supreme value. To have compared the integrative process taking place within him, and the emergence of his own 'myth' with the production of a work of art would have seemed to Jung to denigrate his revelation.

Second, in his writings about artists, which are mostly to be found in Vol. 15 of the Collected Works, 'The Spirit in Man, Art, and Literature', Jung specifically excluded considerations of artistic form, of 'aesthetics', from his discussion, as being beyond the range of psychology. He confines himself to examining the content of literary productions, for instance, and neglects to examine that which makes them into works of art, that is, their style and form. It appears that Jung thought of this aspect of creation as being *consciously* determined, whilst content (at least in the kind of work which interested him) emerged from the unconscious. Hence he was particularly interested in creative works which were often rather naïve 'phantasies from the unconscious' and lacked aesthetic value, like Rider Haggard's 'She'. Yet the evidence is that form, as well as content, is largely determined by unconscious forces. Hence Anton Ehrenzweig names his book on creativity 'The Hidden Order of Art', thereby acknowledging that there is an automatic, pattern-making, ordering activity which is at least partly determined by forces beyond the conscious control of the artist.

As we have seen, the production of mandala patterns became for Jung a symbolic expression of having reached a new synthesis within himself, a conjunction of conscious and unconscious, of phantasy and external reality, of thought and feeling. Because this experience was so intensely important to him, he felt obliged to describe it in religious terms, and so the mandala became a kind of symbolic representation of the archetype of God. Considering Jung's predilection for personifying unconscious contents, it is remarkable that the most important archetype of all should appear, not as a person, but as an abstract pattern. It is at least as convincing to regard a mandala as a rudimentary work of art as it is to look upon it as a religious symbol of the deity. For works of art also represent a new synthesis between the inner, subjective world of the artist and external reality. The artist selects, often unconsciously, material both from external and internal reality, and the work embodies and portrays a conjunction between the two. Moreover, there is clear evidence that artists are more divided in nature than most people, and that one force which drives them to be productive is the need to heal the split. Like Jung's advanced patients, artists are in a special category; more tormented than most, but by virtue of possessing strong egos, more able to cope with and to integrate their own disorder.

When an artist paints a landscape for example, he is portraying both external reality, and his own subjective vision of this reality. He is also arranging his perception within a limited 'frame', within which he is concerned to make a satisfying pattern. This pattern usually consists of a balance between opposing masses, lines of tension, and other 'opposites'. As Harrison Gough has put it: 'A creative product must give a sense of reconciliation, of having resolved in an aesthetic and harmonious way the discords and disharmonies present in the original situation. The work of art, for example, for a moment reorders and brings into balance the tensions of form and space, and in so doing, moderates the inner tensions of the observer, giving him a sense of encounter and fulfilment.'[13]

Suzanne Langer, in 'Feeling and Form'[14] reached the same conclusion about mandalas as Jung from an entirely different angle. It is usual to regard these patterns as originating from attempts to portray circular forms in the external world, but she concludes, like Jung, that they are primary patterns taking origin from within the psyche. Moreover, there is evidence from the work of Rhoda Kellog that children's drawings regularly take on mandala form which she considers to be the most important single unit of pre-representational drawing.

This is not the place to elaborate further the function of art as an integrating, healing process. The reader who is interested is referred to the writings of Ehrenzweig,[15]

Koestler,[16] and to my own book 'The Dynamics of Creation'.[17] What I wanted to make clear was that Jung, in describing the process of individuation and the reconciling of opposites was calling attention to a symbolic process of healing which is of great importance and interest, but which might have been expressed in terms quite other than those which he chose to employ. Jung referred to religions as psychotherapeutic systems. He might equally well have used the same phrase about works of art. Nowadays, more people gain what Jung would have called experience of the Self from one or other of the arts than they do from religion. The picture gallery and the concert hall have replaced the Church as places where the 'divine' can be encountered. There is, throughout the works of Jung, remarkably little reference to any of the arts save literature, with the exception of his essay on Picasso. Wagner interested Jung, because of his use of mythology in the 'Ring', and the religious symbolism of 'Parsifal'. But there is hardly a mention of the work of other musicians. One cannot escape the conclusion that in Jung's scheme of things, the arts ranked very low compared with religious experience.

To my mind, the importance of Jung's description of the process of individuation and the experience of the Self lies in the fact that he recognized that, for many intelligent and able people, the attainment of Freud's goals of 'honour, power, wealth, fame, and the love of women' are not enough. Jung's recognition and delineation of the inner world of the psyche did not include a statement as to why man was so constituted that what went on inside him was so often at variance with the external world that he could not find all his satisfactions therein. But he recognized that man, the symbolic animal, could resolve even the deepest divisions within him upon the symbolic plane; and he invented a technique of psychotherapy by which this could be accomplished. Jung's contributions to the art of psychotherapy are the subject of the next chapter.

One rather odd consequence of Jung's preoccupation with the union of opposites is his notion of synchronicity. Throughout his life, Jung was preoccupied with what he called 'meaningful coincidences', and, as we have seen, with the relation between the inner world of the psyche and the external world. At times he seems to go so far as to postulate a 'third world' in which 'psychoid' events occur which are neither external or internal but which somehow partake of both. This world is equivalent to the Gnostic 'pleroma'; 'the abode of God and of the totality of the Divine powers and emanations'. As we have seen, Jung was little interested in the causal interpretation of mental disorder by tracing the origin of neurotic symptoms to early childhood, as did Freud. It is not surprising, therefore, that he came to believe that there was an acausal principle, of equal importance with causality, which linked events by their coincidence in time rather than sequentially. This concept of synchronicity was compared by Jung with the Chinese concept of 'Tao'. As Koestler has pointed out, some kind of belief in the fundamental unity of all things is a recurrent theme in the history of human thought, and has begun to reappear in the speculations of modern physicists. The reader who wishes to pursue Jung's ideas on synchronicity is referred first to his introduction to the 'I Ching' which occurs in the 11th Volume of the Collected Works, 'Psychology and Religion', and then to Koestler's critique in 'The Roots of Coincidence'.[18] Believers in ghosts, spiritualism, and astrology seize upon this aspect of Jung's thought with avidity; but I must confess that his writings upon synchronicity seem to me to be both confused and of little practical value.

No introduction to Jung's thought would be complete without reference to the art of psychotherapy of which he was so notable a practitioner. Many of his ideas have in fact been incorporated into the schemata advanced by others, although Jung's contribution is seldom acknowledged. This is not, I think, because his ideas have been dishonestly misappropriated, but simply because people find Jung difficult to grasp. As he said himself: 'Nobody reads my books,' and 'I have such a hell of a trouble to make people see what I mean.' For instance, the endpoint of the individuation process, or something very like it, appears as 'self-actualization' or 'self-realization' in the phraseology of other psychologists, and so do some of his views on dreams.

Jung was the first person to insist that the analyst himself be analysed, although for many years he resisted the idea of setting up a formal school of training based on his ideas. He also introduced a number of modifications of analytic technique. In the early days of Freudian psychoanalysis, the total length of analyses varied considerably, most being very much shorter than those which are now common. But the technique of psychoanalysts became somewhat formalized fairly rapidly, so that, for instance, it became *de rigueur* to see patients five times a week, and to insist on their lying on a couch with the analyst out of sight. There are in fact some good reasons for adopting both procedures, but technical arguments about the different approaches of the various schools are out of place in this context. Jung disliked the use of the couch because he felt that it interfered with his direct, face-to-face contact with the patient. He also saw patients much less frequently than the Freudians; four times a week as a maximum, but often only twice a week or once, depending upon the stage which the patient had reached. Interruptions, or 'holidays' from analysis were also frequent.

Jung states that he never wanted his patients to lose contact with their ordinary day-to-day lives during analysis, perhaps recalling how his own professional work and relations with his family had preserved him from breakdown during the years of the first World War. That he was not always successful in achieving this aim is not necessarily Jung's fault. Every experienced psychotherapist knows that there are patients who, partly because their external lives are impoverished, make analysis into a way of life and a substitute for both achievement and human relationships. There are inevitably a number of adherents of both the Freudian and the Jungian schools whose lives are entirely circumscribed by analysis, and who have few contacts outside analytical circles. For such people, the Jungian camp has more to offer; for the possibilities of scholarly research along Jungian lines are much more ample than those provided by Freudian psychoanalysis.

In recent years, many Freudian analysts have become much more flexible about how often they see patients, and some make little use of the couch, though most continue to find this technical procedure useful. Jung anticipated this move towards greater flexibility by many years.

I have already commented upon the fact that Jung was less interested in the past than in the present and the future of the patient's development. In this sense he resembled Adler more than Freud, for Adler laid a great emphasis upon the goal towards which the patient was aiming. Jung has been much criticized for his 'teleological' view-point; but I think that he is actually more vulnerable to attack for his neglect of the patient's personal childhood. This may be more apparent than real; but the fact remains that many neurotic symptoms are more easily comprehended in terms of the patient's childhood experience and misapprehensions than in terms of the Jungian mechanism of compensation. It is, for example, difficult to interpret agoraphobia as a compensatory symptom; but easy to understand it in terms of a persistence of childhood dependency. This is, of course, not to deny the importance of Jung's idea of self-regulation and compensation; but only to point out that it does not apply universally without distortion.

Jung believed that the cause of neurosis was to be found in the present and not in the past. Patients became neurotic when they got 'stuck', as he called it; that is, when they no longer pursued the natural path of psychological development which takes place with ageing. This getting stuck was generally due to an evasion of one of the 'obligations' in life to which Jung makes frequent reference. Thus, a man who always runs away from women, or a woman who invariably evades motherhood, might find themselves becoming neurotic because of their lack of courage. Jung recognized that, under such conditions, patients present much infantile material, including incestuous desires, infantile sexuality, and all the other childhood phantasies with which Freudian psychoanalysis has made us familiar. But, unlike Freud, Jung considered that the emergence of this material was secondary to something wrong in the present. It was only when a person's libidinal energy was not finding its proper expression in the here-and-now that his infantile phantasies became regressively reactivated. Whereas Freud conceived of his patients as being held up in the present by their inability to free themselves from their fixations upon the past, Jung believed that their regression to past fixations derived from their block in the present. Both points of view have a good deal to be said for them. Every psychotherapist will be familiar with patients who have never grown up, and thus correspond with Freud's description. On the other hand, there is a tendency amongst Freudian analysts to confine their interest in the patient's infantile past to the exclusion of considering his adaptation in the present: and psychoanalysis often fails to give a satisfactory answer to the problem of why, if infantile fixations are the cause of a patient's symptoms, they should suddenly cause these symptoms to become troublesome at the particular time in adult life at which they do so.

Jung often paid tribute to Freud for the latter's revolutionary discovery that dreams were the 'royal road' to the unconscious. However, he came to disagree with Freud's view of dreams in many important respects. Jung did not accept the idea that dreams were invariably concealing the unacceptable; that is, that there was a 'manifest content' cloaking a 'latent content', which usually turned out to be an infantile wish-fulfilment. Nor did he accept the idea that dreams necessarily took origin from the dreamer's childhood. I have already commented upon Jung's valuable notion of the compensatory function of the unconscious, and given an example of how a dream can serve as a counterbalance to the conscious attitude (in Chapter 1). This point of view implies that dreams are at least as much concerned with the dreamer's state of mind at the time of dreaming as with the past. The psychoanalyst Fairbairn came to a rather similar conclusion when he abandoned the wish-fulfilment theory in favour of the view that dreams are dramatizations of situations existing in the patient's inner world. Jung regarded the language of dreams as a natural, symbolic language which might be difficult to understand, but which was not an attempt to conceal anything. He tried to read dreams as one might approach an unknown foreign tongue. In interpreting a dream, Jung asked for his patient's associations to each image which appeared in it. Whereas a Freudian analyst would encourage 'free association' which might lead away from the dream to other emotional preoccupations, Jung asked his patients to confine their associations more closely to the dream images themselves. As he pointed out, free association will invariably lead eventually to the patient's problems, whether the associations start from a dream or from a fly on the wall of the consulting room. But free association in itself will not explain the dream, and may often result in both patient and analyst failing to interpret it at all.

In Jung's view, many dreams originated from the 'personal unconscious' of the patient; that is, were concerned with his day-to-day emotional problems, with interpersonal relationships, with childhood residues; in fact, with the tangles deriving from family interaction with which Freud has familiarized us. What interested Jung, however, were the dreams which appeared to him to originate from the 'collective unconscious'. As we have seen, Freud also recognized that some dreams brought to light material which could not have originated from the dreamer's adult life or from his forgotten childhood (see Chapter 1). To the mythological images in such dreams the patient could not be expected to have any personal associations, and might not have any associations at all. In such instances, Jung did not hesitate to supply his own associations, culled from his own extensive knowledge of mythology, comparative religion, and alchemy. In 'Psychology and Alchemy' Jung interprets a series of dreams dreamed by a patient whom he saw only once and then sent to a colleague. Of the four hundred dreams and visions which Jung examined, only forty-five occurred under his direct observation. For reasons of discretion, Jung excludes from the series the dreams which brought up details of the patient's personal life, and so the reader is apt to be left with the false impression that this particular patient dreamed nothing but 'collective dreams'. In fact, many of the dreams quoted would be very difficult to understand without employing Jung's technique of 'amplification', as his practice of supplying analogies and comparisons is named. But the critical reader may often feel that Jung's interpretations are somewhat arbitrary, and that, if he possessed as much knowledge as did Jung, he might venture upon another set of interpretations of equally convincing validity. However, this 'if' is a formidable obstacle, for very few people do know as much about mythology and religion as Jung did, and fewer still have studied alchemy or Chinese Yoga. One of the principal difficulties in producing a scholarly critique of Jung, (and it is a task which some scholar ought to undertake) is that to do so requires a knowledge of many subjects with which only specialists are familiar.

In ordinary psychotherapeutic practice, dreams of an unequivocally collective nature are comparatively rare. When they do occur, however, they have precisely the 'numinous', impressive quality which Jung describes, and many people will remember at least one example of such a dream from their own experience. For example, a man dreamed that he had to enter a mysterious house, half buried beneath the sands of the sea-shore, in which was concealed a treasure; a golden ring which he had to obtain. After accomplishing this, he emerged on the shore where he observed that the sea was crowded with a vast number of whales, each suckling their young. The mythological quality of such a dream is obvious, and the theme of the buried treasure, the sea, and the maternal 'monsters' are all archetypal, and recognizable in myth and fairytale. It would certainly be possible to interpret a dream of this kind in 'personal' terms if one knew the dreamer well, and had his associations to it. But it is also surely permissible, indeed inescapable, to compare the dream images with their counterparts in, for example, Wagner's 'Ring of the Nibelungs'.

Jung was, I think, inclined to see collective material in dreams which could equally well be looked upon as merely personal. Like every creative person, he sometimes oversold his own discoveries. But his view of dreams has a great deal to commend it, and is often fruitful in clinical practice. He does offer a method for understanding dreams which are obviously mythological which is unmatched by psychoanalysis. Moreover, he understood the difference between a sign and a symbol in a way which Freud did not. When Freud alleged, as he did in 'The Interpretation of Dreams', that all weapons and tools are used as symbols for the male organ, he might equally well have used the word 'sign' instead of symbol. In Jung's view, a symbol was more than this. A true symbol always possesses overtones, so that its full significance cannot be grasped intellectually, at least immediately. If it becomes fully definable in rational terms, it is no longer a living symbol. Jung, characteristically enough, gives as an example of what he means the Christian Cross. For St. Paul, and for the early mystics, the Cross stood for something which could not be clearly defined, but which was of immense importance. As time went on, the Cross no longer bore the same significance. In the same way, one might say that it is unlikely that, for most people, the music of Palestrina has the same significance as it did for his contemporaries, and one might have the same difficulty in defining the exact meaning of his, or any other composer's, music as one has in defining the meaning of the Cross for the early Christians. A work of art is a true symbol in the Jungian sense, in that it is pregnant with meaning, partakes of both 'conscious' and 'unconscious', yet cannot be sharply defined in purely intellectual terms.

Moreover, Freud's view of symbols as mere disguises fails to explain why the same man may dream of a dagger or an umbrella on one occasion, and the penis undisguised upon another. Freud treated parts of the body, and more especially the genitals, as bedrock reality to which all else must be reduced. Yet parts of the body can themselves be used to signify something other than their usual function. The male genitals, for example, were used by the Romans and others as a magical threat to warn off intruders, and may be seen on Hadrian's Wall pointing towards the enemy. It is alleged, probably apocryphally, that Jung once stated: 'After all, the penis is only a phallic symbol.' Even if he did not say this, the remark aptly illustrates the point that, for Jung, the psychological was just as 'real' as the physical. The same could not be said of Freud.

Jung also made a contribution to the concept of transference. Students of psychoanalysis are familiar with the idea that the patient projects upon the analyst images derived from his experience of significant figures from the past; very often, of course, parental figures, but sometimes other people as well. The more the analyst is an unknown figure, the more likely are images from the patient's inner world to become attached to him. It is the unknown person sitting opposite to us who stimulates our speculative imagination; not the friend with whose actual character and circumstances we are familiar. Jung added to the Freudian conception of transference his observation that it was not only personal images from the patient's childhood which became projected, but also archetypal figures of the kind discussed in Chapter 3. This, Jung believed, was especially true of those patients who had largely worked through their boring personal problems, and had progressed to the stage of embarking upon the real thing, the process of individuation. The simplest account of how archetypal images of gods, devils, and the like can become projected upon the analyst is to be found in Vol 7 of the Collected Works, 'Two Essays on Analytical Psychology'. Analysts of other schools are familiar with the same phenomenon, but refer to it in different terminology. Kleinians, for example, would certainly recognize these images of wholly 'good' and entirely 'bad' figures, but would attribute their projection to a persistence of, or a profound regression to, the 'paranoid-schizoid' stage of emotional development, which they believe to be characteristic of the earliest stage of infancy. As a matter of clinical experience, the projection of such figures upon oneself as an analyst is somewhat alarming, more especially when the good and bad aspects alternate rapidly. Such a phenomenon sometimes presages a psychotic breakdown, and may demand the cessation of analysis, or the patient's admission to hospital. But Jung's patients who dreamed of him as God, magician, or devil were, if not entirely free of symptoms, at least well-embarked upon the analytical journey towards integration. This is a paradox which requires explanation. It may be understood in one of two ways. Either Jung was so expert an analyst that he could induce even fairly well-adjusted persons to penetrate the recesses of the unconscious so thoroughly that they reached this 'deep' or 'early' material without undue disturbance, or else the people whom he describes were an unusual group. I think it probable that both explanations are true.

In addition to describing the projection of archetypal figures in the transference, Jung made another contribution, 'Psychology of the Transference', which is to be found in Vol. 16 of the Collected Works. This is a late work, not easily grasped by those not already familiar with Jungian thought. Nevertheless, its central theme is both interesting and important. The alchemists expressed their notion of integration, the coming together of opposites, in terms of an incestuous union between the sexes, who were not only related, but also royal. As Freud rightly discerned, transference projections are 'incestuous', in that the patient tends to treat the analyst both as parent and potential lover simultaneously. Whereas Freud interpreted this phenomenon as the persistence of an infantile attitude which ought to have been outgrown, Jung interpreted it as a symbolic attempt of the patient to reach a new kind of integration within his own personality. Just as the penis can symbolize aggression or regal power (e.g. the sceptre), so sexual intercourse can symbolize the integration of the personality and the experience of the irrational union of opposites. This view will no doubt seem incomprehensible to those for whom sexual intercourse is the most important experience in life. Others, differently constituted, who find their supreme value in religion, in scientific discovery, or in art, will more easily comprehend Jung's meaning. Again, such an interpretation of the transference is probably only appropriate to persons in the second half of life who have worked through human relationships and discovered that, for them, salvation lies elsewhere.

I have made frequent reference to the fact that the patients who most interested Jung were a special group, rather unlike the usual run of neurotics. For this group, Jung developed a new technique, which is known as 'active imagination'. During his own self-analysis, Jung had drawn and painted his own visions and dreams. He encouraged his patients to do likewise; or, if they preferred it, to write poems, make models or sculptures, or even to dance their phantasies. Although a patient might treat a dream in this fashion, and would be encouraged to do so, Jung was more particularly interested in the kind of phantasy which comes to people when they are neither awake nor asleep, but in a state of reverie in which judgement is suspended, but consciousness is not lost. Those who are familiar with the accounts given by creative people of how they happened upon their discoveries, will recognize that it is in just this state of reverie that inspiration is most commonly reputed to occur. Although some ideas or solutions to problems may come to the creator through dreams, it is more usual for inspiration to appear in the half-waking state, as, for instance, Wagner reports when he describes his discovery of the opening bars of 'Das Rheingold'. The technique of active imagination, therefore, was one which deliberately mobilized the patient's creativity. As Jung wrote himself : 'What the doctor then does is less a question of treatment than of developing the creative possibilities latent in the patient himself.'[1]

As we have seen, Jung was particularly impatient with the idea that his own drawings and paintings were in any sense works of art : and he firmly discouraged his patients from considering their own productions as works of art either, however beautiful they might appear. Nevertheless, when Jung is describing the process of individuation and the technique of active imagination which bridges the gap between conscious and unconscious, he is describing the creative process in identical language to that used by artists and inventors.

In recent years, the use of painting, music, and modelling as a therapeutic tool in mental hospitals and clinics has increased, and the healing effect of creative endeavour, however technically inept, has become more generally recognized. Jung's influence in bringing about this valuable change has been underestimated, in common with his other contributions to psychotherapeutic technique.

A Personal Postscript

Jung died only in 1961. It is therefore premature to assess the ultimate importance of his contribution to our conception of human nature. My personal view is that this has so far been underestimated; and that the neglect of Jung has been chiefly because of his inability to express himself in easily comprehensible terms. In the field of writing, Freud had an enormous advantage. Indeed, Freud wrote with such clarity and conviction that he is apt to still criticism and over-convince the reader. Jung, with his emphasis upon the spiritual, as opposed to the physical, aspects of human nature, provides an important and necessary counterbalance to Freud's obsession with the body. It is easy to lose patience with Jung, as I have myself at times. More especially, I find it difficult to sympathize with his preoccupation with the occult; with his views on synchronicity, and with the ghosts and poltergeists which throng his autobiography. But his ideas on extraversion and introversion, his notion of a self-regulating psyche, his description of the process of individuation, and his belief that the divisions in man can be healed in symbolic fashion, are profoundly valuable. If this short introduction to Jung's ideas helps to stimulate further interest in them, and to bridge the wide gap which has hitherto existed between Jung's concepts and the ideas of others, it will have fulfilled the purpose I had in mind when writing it.

Biographical Note

C. G. Jung was born at Kesswil, Canton Thurgau, Switzerland, on July 26th, 1875. He became a medical student at the University of Basel.

In 1900, having decided to specialize in psychiatry, he obtained a post at the Burghölzli mental hospital at Zürich. During 1902 his first publication appeared and, in 1905, he was appointed lecturer in psychiatry at the University of Zürich.

Quick to perceive the value of Freud's early work, Jung was one of the first psychiatrists to apply psychoanalytic ideas to the study of insanity. In 1906 he published 'The Psychology of Dementia Praecox', a psychoanalytic interpretation of schizophrenia. He sent the book to Freud, and consequently went to meet Freud at Vienna in March 1907. There followed some six years of collaboration.

In 1909 Jung resigned his post at the Burghölzli in favour of his growing private practice, and, in the same year, travelled with Freud to the USA to lecture at Clark University. Increasing divergences between the two men led to their final separation in 1913.

1913 also saw the publication of Jung's 'Psychology of the Unconscious'. This was the first of his books which makes manifest his individual point of view and the difference between psychoanalysis and 'analytical psychology', as Jung's psychology was henceforth known.

During the years 1913–17, Jung went through a period of mental turmoil in which he conducted a self-analysis and finally abandoned a conventional career by resigning his lectureship at the University of Zürich. The end of this disturbed period was marked by the writing of one of his major works, 'Psychological Types', which was published in 1921 and greatly increased his reputation.

The remainder of his life was outwardly uneventful, although the routine of his private practice was interrupted by travels to India, Africa, the USA, and other parts of the world. 1937 was notable for his delivery of the Terry Lectures, 'Psychology and Religion' at Yale University.

For most of his life Jung lived in the same house at Küsnacht on the lakeside of Zürich. He died on June 6th, 1961, at the age of eighty-five.

Jung was a prolific writer, as the eighteen volumes of the Collected Works attest.

References

CW   *Collected Works*, London: Routledge and Kegan Paul, 1953–71

MDR *Memories, Dreams, Reflections*, London: Routledge and Kegan Paul, 1963 and Collins/Fontana, 1967. References are to both editions in the order shown here

TL   *Analytical Psychology: its Theory and Practice.* The Tavistock Lectures. London: Routledge and Kegan Paul, 1963

CHAPTER 1

1. *MDR*, Routledge 213; Fontana 251
2. Freud, Sigmund. *An Outline of Psycho-Analysis.* Standard Edition, vol. XXIII. London: The Hogarth Press and Institute of Psycho-Analysis, 1964, 166–7
3. *MDR*, Routledge 170; Fontana 200
4. *MDR*, Routledge 181; Fontana 213
5. Storr, Anthony. *The Dynamics of Creation*, London: Martin Secker and Warburg, 1972
6. *MDR*, Routledge 191; Fontana 225
7. Jaques, Elliott. 'Death and the Mid-Life Crisis' in *Work, Creativity and Social Justice*, London: Heinemann, 1970, 38–63

CHAPTER 2

1. *TL*, 80–1
2. Freud, Standard Edition, XII, 71
3. *CW*, Vol. 3, 189
4. *MDR*, Routledge 237; Fontana 280
5. *CW*, 8, 150

CHAPTER 3

1. *CW*, 9, Part 1, 79

2. Donington, Robert. *Wagner's Ring: its Musical and Mythological Symbols*, London: Faber and Faber, 1963
3. Storr, *The Dynamics of Creation*
4. *CW*, 5, 261
5. *CW*, 4, 321 note
6. *CW*, 4, 321 note
7. *CW*, 4, 320
8. Lorenz, Konrad. *Evolution and Modification of Behaviour*, London: Methuen, 1966, 25
9. *CW*, 7, 188
10. *CW*, 7, 208
11. *CW*, 3, 26
12. *MDR*, Routledge 327; Fontana 388
13. Masters, R. E. L. and Houston, J. *The Varieties of Psychedelic Experience*, London: Blond, 1967
14. *CW*, 9, Part 1, 262

CHAPTER 4
1. *CW*, 6, 499
2. *CW*, 7, 41
3. *CW*, 6, 16
4. *CW*, 7, 43
5. *TL*, 11–12
6. *TL*, 17
7. 'Face to Face,' BBC Script, 1959

CHAPTER 5
1. *CW*, 13, 14
2. Fenichel, Otto. *The Psycho-Analytic Theory of Neurosis*, London: Routledge and Kegan Paul, 1947, 19
3. *CW*, 16, 41
4. *CW*, 16, 41
5. Freud, Standard Edition, XVI, 376
6. *CW*, 13, 46
7. *CW*, 13, 47–8
8. Taylor, F. Sherwood. *The Alchemists*, London: Heinemann, 1951

CHAPTER 6

 1. *CW*, 13, 15
 2. *CW*, 13, 15
 3. *CW*, 7, 188
 4. *CW*, 12, 10–11
 5. *CW*, 13, 38
 6. *CW*, 11, 357–8
 7. White, Victor. *God and the Unconscious*, London: Harvill Press, 1952
 8. Hostie, Raymond. *Religion and the Psychology of Jung*, London: Sheed and Ward, 1957
 9. *CW*, 16, 80
10. *MDR*, Routledge 179–80; Fontana 211–12
11. *MDR*, Routledge 187; Fontana 220–1
12. Wallas, Graham. *The Art of Thought*, London: Cape, 1926
13. Gough, Harrison. *Identifying the Creative Man*, Journal of Value Engineering, Vol. 2, no. 4, Aug. 15 1964, 5–12
14. Langer, Suzanne. *Feeling and Form*, London: Routledge and Kegan Paul, 1953, 69–70
15. Ehrenzweig, Anton. *The Hidden Order of Art*, London: Weidenfeld and Nicolson, 1967
16. Koestler, Arthur. *The Act of Creation*, London: Hutchinson, 1964
17. Storr, *The Dynamics of Creation*
18. Koestler, Arthur. *The Roots of Coincidence*, London: Hutchinson, 1972

CHAPTER 7

 1. *CW*, 16, 41

Books on Jung and
Analytical Psychology

Jung, C. G., *Collected Works*, vols. 1–20. London: Routledge and Kegan Paul, 1953–79

Jung, C. G., *Letters*, ed. Gerhard Adler, vols. 1–2. London: Routledge and Kegan Paul, 1973 and 1976

Jung, C. G., *Memories, Dreams, Reflections*. London: Collins and Routledge and Kegan Paul, 1963; Collins/Fontana, 1967

Jung, C. G., von Franz, Marie-Louise, Henderson, J. L., Jacobi, Jolande, Jaffé, Aniela, *Man and His Symbols*. London: Aldus Books, 1964; Picador (Pan), 1978

Jung, C. G., *Septem Sermones ad Mortuos*. London: John M. Watkins, 1967

Jaffé, Aniela, ed., *C. G. Jung: Word and Image*. Princeton University Press, 1979

McGuire, William, ed., *The Freud/Jung Letters*. London: The Hogarth Press and Routledge and Kegan Paul, 1974

McGuire, William and Hull, R. F. C., eds., *C. G. Jung Speaking: Interviews and Encounters*. Princeton University Press, 1977; London: Thames and Hudson, 1978; Picador, 1980

Adler, Gerhard, *Studies in Analytical Psychology*. London: Routledge and Kegan Paul, 1948

Bennet, E. A., *C. G. Jung*. London: Barrie and Rockcliffe, 1961

Bennet, E. A., *What Jung Really Said*. London: Macdonald, 1966

Brome, Vincent, *Jung: Man and Myth*. London: Macmillan, 1978

Dry, Avis M., *The Psychology of Jung*. London: Methuen, 1962

Fordham, Frieda, *An Introduction to Jung's Psychology*. Harmondsworth: Pelican, 1953

Hannah, Barbara, *Jung: His Life and Work*. New York: G. P. Putnam's Sons, 1976

Hostie, Raymond, *Religion and the Psychology of Jung*. London: Sheed and Ward, 1957

Moreno, Antonio, *Jung, Gods and Modern Man*. London: Sheldon Press, 1974

Odajnyk, Volodymyr Walter, *Jung and Politics*. New York: Harper and Row, 1976

Papadopoulos, Renos K. and Saayman, Graham S., *Jung in Modern Perspective*. London: Wildwood House, 1984

Samuels, Andrew, *Jung and the Post-Jungians*. London: Routledge and Kegan Paul, 1985

Serrano, Miguel, *C. G. Jung & Hermann Hesse: A Record of Two Friendships*. New York: Schocken, 1968

Staude, John-Raphael, *The Adult Development of C. G. Jung*. London: Routledge and Kegan Paul, 1981

Stern, Paul J., *C. G. Jung: the Haunted Prophet*. New York: Braziller, 1976

Von Franz, Marie-Louise, *C. G. Jung: His Myth in Our Time*. New York: G. P. Putnam's Sons for the C. G. Jung Foundation for Analytical Psychology, 1975

Von Franz, Marie-Louise, *Number and Time*. London: Rider, 1975

White, Victor, *God and the Unconscious*. London: Harvill, 1952